Classic Brand Name
GRANDMA'S
COOKIE JAR
COOKBOOK

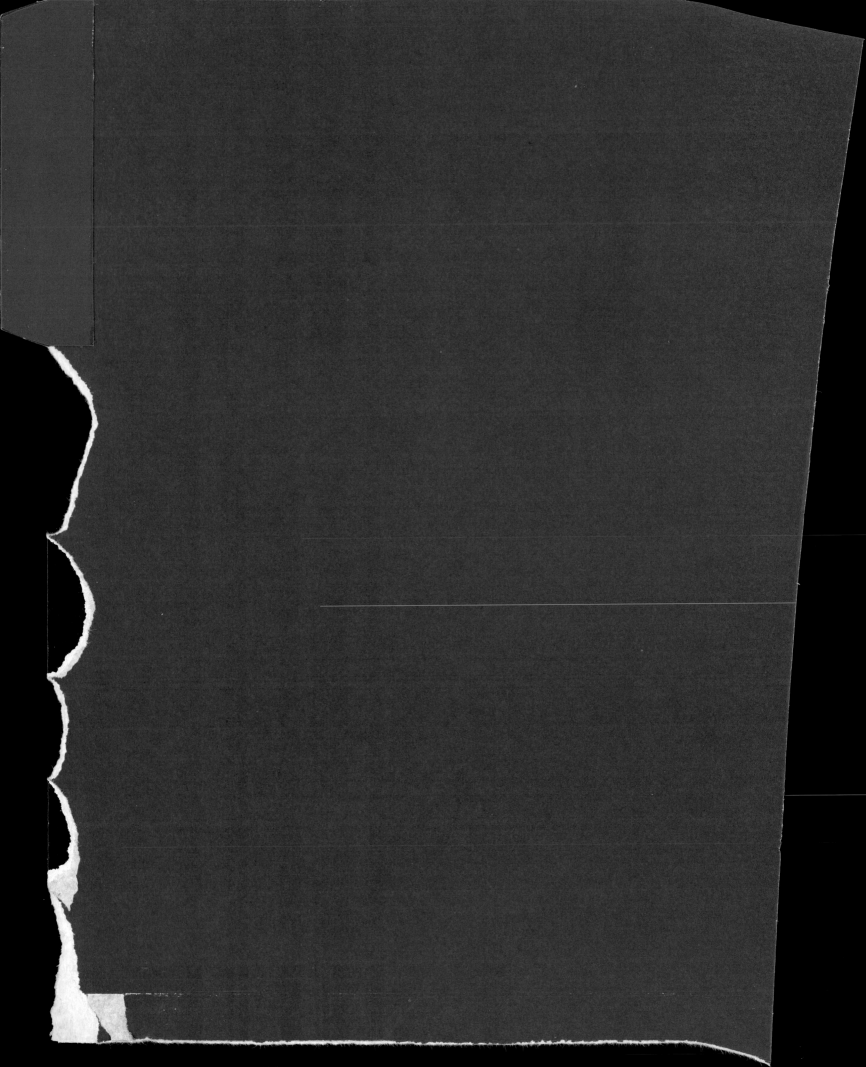

Classic Brand Name

GRANDMA'S

COOKIE JAR

COOKBOOK

ALL-TIME FAVORITES

ALMOND–ORANGE SHORTBREAD

1 cup (4 ounces) sliced almonds, divided
2 cups all-purpose flour
1 cup cold butter, cut into pieces
½ cup sugar
½ cup cornstarch
2 tablespoons grated orange peel
1 teaspoon almond extract

1. Preheat oven to 350°F. Spread ¾ cup almonds in single layer in large baking pan. Bake 6 minutes or until golden brown, stirring frequently. Cool completely in pan. *Reduce oven temperature to 325°F.*

2. Place toasted almonds in food processor. Process using on/off pulsing action until almonds are coarsely chopped.

3. Add flour, butter, sugar, cornstarch, orange peel and almond extract to food processor. Process using on/off pulsing action until mixture resembles coarse crumbs.

4. Press dough firmly and evenly into 10×8½-inch rectangle on large ungreased cookie sheet with fingers. Score dough into 1¼-inch squares with knife. Press one slice of remaining almonds in center of each square.

5. Bake 30 to 40 minutes or until shortbread is firm when pressed and lightly browned. Immediately cut into squares along score lines with sharp knife. Remove cookies to wire racks; cool completely.

6. Store loosely covered at room temperature up to 1 week.

Makes about 5 dozen cookies

Almond-Orange Shortbread

FUDGY RAISIN PIXIES

½ cup butter, softened
2 cups granulated sugar
4 eggs
2 cups all-purpose flour, divided
¾ cup unsweetened cocoa powder
2 teaspoons baking powder
½ teaspoon salt
½ cup chocolate-covered raisins
   Powdered sugar

Beat butter and granulated sugar in large bowl until light and fluffy. Add eggs; mix until well blended. Combine 1 cup flour, cocoa, baking powder and salt in small bowl; add to butter mixture. Mix until well blended. Stir in remaining 1 cup flour and chocolate-covered raisins. Cover; refrigerate until firm, 2 hours or overnight.

Preheat oven to 350°F. Grease cookie sheets. Coat hands with powdered sugar. Shape rounded teaspoonfuls of dough into 1-inch balls; roll in powdered sugar. Place 2 inches apart on prepared cookie sheets. Bake 14 to 17 minutes or until firm to the touch. Remove immediately from cookie sheets; cool completely on wire racks.

Makes about 4 dozen cookies

OATMEAL SCOTCHIES

1 cup (2 sticks) margarine or butter, softened
¾ cup granulated sugar
¾ cup firmly packed brown sugar
2 eggs
1 teaspoon vanilla *or* 2 teaspoons grated orange peel (about 1 orange)
1¼ cups all-purpose flour
1 teaspoon baking soda
½ teaspoon salt (optional)
½ teaspoon ground cinnamon
3 cups QUAKER® Oats (quick or old fashioned, uncooked)
1 (12-ounce) package (2 cups) NESTLE® TOLL HOUSE® Butterscotch Flavored Morsels

Heat oven to 375°F. Beat together margarine, sugars, eggs and vanilla until creamy. Gradually add combined flour, baking soda, salt and cinnamon; mix well. Stir in remaining ingredients. Drop by level measuring tablespoonfuls onto ungreased cookie sheet. Bake 7 to 8 minutes for a chewy cookie or 9 to 10 minutes for a crisp cookie. Cool 2 minutes on cookie sheet; remove to wire rack. Cool completely.

Makes about 4 dozen cookies

CHOCOLATE CHIP COOKIES

8 tablespoons margarine, softened
1½ cups packed light brown sugar
2 egg whites
1 teaspoon vanilla
2½ cups all-purpose flour
1½ teaspoons baking soda
½ teaspoon salt
⅓ cup fat-free (skim) milk
¾ cup (4 ounces) semisweet chocolate chips
½ cup chopped pecans or walnuts (optional)

1. Preheat oven to 350°F. Spray cookie sheets with nonstick cooking spray.

2. Beat margarine and brown sugar in large bowl until fluffy. Beat in egg whites and vanilla.

3. Combine flour, baking soda and salt in medium bowl. Add flour mixture to margarine mixture alternately with milk, ending with flour mixture. Stir in chocolate chips and pecans.

4. Drop dough by slightly rounded tablespoonfuls onto prepared cookie sheets. Bake about 10 minutes or until lightly browned. Cool on wire racks.

Makes about 6 dozen cookies

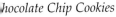

Chocolate Chip Cookies

Holiday Sugar Cookies

1 cup butter, softened
¾ cup sugar
1 egg
2 cups all-purpose flour
1 teaspoon baking powder
¼ teaspoon ground cinnamon
¼ teaspoon salt
   Colored sprinkles or sugar, for
      decorating (optional)

Beat butter and sugar in large bowl with electric mixer until creamy. Add egg; beat until fluffy.

Stir in flour, baking powder, cinnamon and salt until well blended. Form dough into a ball; wrap in plastic wrap and flatten. Refrigerate about 2 hours or until firm.

Preheat oven to 350°F. Roll out dough, a small portion at a time, to ¼-inch thickness on lightly floured surface with lightly floured rolling pin. (Keep remaining dough wrapped in refrigerator.)

Cut out cookies with 3-inch cookie cutter. Sprinkle with colored sprinkles or sugar, if desired. Transfer to ungreased cookie sheets.

Bake 7 to 9 minutes until edges are lightly browned. Let cookies stand on cookie sheets 1 minute; transfer to wire racks to cool completely. Store in airtight container.

Makes about 3 dozen cookies

Chewy Oatmeal Raisin Cookies

1 cup packed light brown sugar
1 cup FLEISCHMANN'S® Original
   Margarine, softened
¼ cup EGG BEATERS® Healthy Real
   Egg Product
1 teaspoon vanilla extract
2 cups quick-cooking oats
1½ cups all-purpose flour
1 teaspoon baking soda
1 teaspoon ground cinnamon
1 cup seedless raisins

1. Beat sugar and margarine in large bowl with mixer at medium speed until blended. Beat in Egg Beaters® and vanilla until mixture is smooth.

2. Blend in oats, flour, baking soda and cinnamon. Stir in raisins.

3. Drop batter by tablespoonfuls, 2 inches apart, onto greased baking sheets. Bake in preheated 400°F oven for 5 to 7 minutes or until lightly browned. Remove from sheets; cool on wire racks.

Makes about 3 dozen cookies

Preparation Time: 25 minutes
Cook Time: 20 minutes

Buttery Almond Cutouts

1 cup butter, softened
1½ cups granulated sugar
¾ cup sour cream
2 eggs
3 teaspoons almond extract, divided
1 teaspoon vanilla
4⅓ cups all-purpose flour
1 teaspoon baking powder
1 teaspoon baking soda
½ teaspoon salt
2 cups powdered sugar
2 tablespoons milk
1 tablespoon light corn syrup
   Food color

1. Beat butter and granulated sugar in large bowl until light and fluffy. Add sour cream, eggs, 2 teaspoons almond extract and vanilla; beat until smooth. Add combined flour, baking powder, baking soda and salt; beat just until well blended.

2. Divide dough into 4 pieces; flatten each piece into disc. Wrap with plastic wrap. Refrigerate at least 3 hours.

3. Combine powdered sugar, milk, corn syrup and remaining 1 teaspoon almond extract in small bowl. Cover and refrigerate.

4. Preheat oven to 375°F. Working with 1 disc at a time, roll dough out onto floured surface to ¼-inch thickness. Cut into desired shapes using 2½-inch cookie cutters. Place about 2 inches apart onto ungreased cookie sheets. Bake 7 to 8 minutes or until edges are firm and bottoms are brown. Remove from cookie sheets to wire rack to cool.

5. Separate powdered sugar mixture into 3 or 4 batches in small bowls; tint each batch with desired food color. Frost cookies.

Makes about 3 dozen cookies

Peanut Butter Chocolate Chip Cookies

¼ cup butter or margarine, softened
¼ cup shortening
½ cup REESE'S® Creamy Peanut Butter
½ cup packed light brown sugar
½ cup granulated sugar
1 egg
1¼ cups all-purpose flour
¾ teaspoon baking soda
½ teaspoon baking powder
2 cups (12-ounce package) HERSHEY'S® Semi-Sweet Chocolate Chips
   Granulated sugar

1. Heat oven to 375°F.

2. Beat butter butter, shortening, peanut butter, brown sugar, ½ cup granulated sugar and egg in large mixer bowl until light and fluffy. Stir together flour, baking soda and baking powder; add to butter mixture. Stir in chocolate chips (if necessary, with hands work chocolate chips into batter).

3. Shape into 1-inch balls; place on ungreased cookie sheet. With fork dipped in granulated sugar flatten slightly in criss-cross pattern.

4. Bake 9 to 11 minutes or just until set. Cool slightly; remove from cookie sheet to wire rack. Cool completely.

Makes about 3 dozen cookies

OATMEAL TOFFEE LIZZIES

¾ **Butter Flavor* CRISCO® Stick or ¾ cup Butter Flavor CRISCO® all-vegetable shortening plus additional for greasing**
1¼ **cups firmly packed light brown sugar**
1 **egg**
⅓ **cup milk**
1½ **teaspoons vanilla extract**
3 **cups quick oats, uncooked**
1 **cup all-purpose flour**
½ **teaspoon baking soda**
½ **teaspoon salt**
1½ **cups semi-sweet chocolate chips**
½ **cup almond brickle chips**
½ **cup finely chopped pecans**

*Butter Flavor Crisco is artificially flavored.

1. Heat oven to 375°F. Grease baking sheets with shortening. Place sheets of foil on countertop for cooling cookies.

2. Combine ¾ cup shortening, brown sugar, egg, milk and vanilla in large bowl. Beat at medium speed of electric mixer until well blended.

3. Combine oats, flour, baking soda and salt. Mix into creamed mixture at low speed just until blended. Stir in chocolate chips, almond chips and pecans.

4. Shape dough into 1¼- to 1½-inch balls with lightly floured hands. Place 2 inches apart onto prepared baking sheet. Flatten slightly.

5. Bake one baking sheet at a time at 375°F for 10 to 12 minutes, or until lightly browned. *Do not overbake.* Cool 2 minutes on baking sheet. Remove cookies to foil to cool completely.
Makes about 2½ dozen cookies

BUTTERY ALMOND COOKIES

1¼ **cups all-purpose flour**
½ **teaspoon baking powder**
⅛ **teaspoon salt**
10 **tablespoons butter, softened**
¾ **cup sugar**
1 **egg**
1 **teaspoon vanilla**
¾ **cup slivered almonds, finely chopped**
½ **cup slivered almonds, for garnish**

Preheat oven to 350°F. Grease cookie sheets. Combine flour, baking powder and salt in small bowl.

Beat butter in large bowl with electric mixer at medium speed until smooth. Gradually beat in sugar until blended; increase speed to high and beat until light and fluffy. Beat in egg until fluffy. Beat in vanilla until blended. Stir in flour mixture until blended. Stir in chopped almonds just until combined.

Drop rounded teaspoonfuls of dough about 2 inches apart onto prepared cookie sheets. Top each cookie with several slivered almonds, pressing into dough.

Bake 12 minutes or until edges are golden brown. Let cookies stand on cookie sheets 5 minutes; transfer to wire racks to cool completely. Store in airtight container.
Makes about 3½ dozen cookies

Buttery Almond Cookies

Hershey's Milk Chocolate Chip Giant Cookies

6 tablespoons butter, softened
½ cup granulated sugar
¼ cup packed light brown sugar
½ teaspoon vanilla extract
1 egg
1 cup all-purpose flour
½ teaspoon baking soda
2 cups (11.5-ounce package) HERSHEY'S Milk Chocolate Chips
Frosting (optional)
Ice cream (optional)

1. Heat oven to 350°F. Line two 9-inch round baking pans with foil, extending foil over edge of pans.

2. Beat butter, granulated sugar, brown sugar and vanilla until light and fluffy. Add egg; beat well. Stir together flour and baking soda; gradually add to butter mixture, beating until well blended. Stir in milk chocolate chips. Spread one half of batter into each prepared pan, spreading to 1 inch from edge. (Cookies will spread to edge when baking.)

3. Bake 15 to 20 minutes or until lightly browned. Cool completely; carefully lift cookies from pans and remove foil. Frost, if desired. Cut each cookie into wedges; serve topped with scoop of ice cream, if desired.

Makes about 12 to 16 servings

Tip: Bake cookies on the middle rack of oven, one pan at a time. Uneven browning can occur if baking on more than one rack at the same time.

Pecan Cookies

1¼ cups confectioners' sugar
1 Butter Flavor* CRISCO® Stick or 1 cup Butter Flavor CRISCO® all-vegetable shortening
2 eggs
¼ cup light corn syrup or regular pancake syrup
1 tablespoon vanilla extract
2 cups all-purpose flour
1½ cups finely chopped pecans
¾ teaspoon baking powder
½ teaspoon baking soda
½ teaspoon salt
Confectioners' sugar

Butter Flavor Crisco is artificially flavored.

1. Heat oven to 350°F. Place sheets of foil on countertop for cooling cookies.

2. Place confectioners' sugar and 1 cup shortening in large bowl. Beat at medium speed of electric mixer until well blended. Add eggs, syrup and vanilla; beat until well blended and fluffy.

3. Combine flour, pecans, baking powder, baking soda and salt. Add to shortening mixture; beat at low speed until well blended.

4. Shape dough into 1-inch balls. Place 2 inches apart on ungreased baking sheet.

5. Bake for 15 to 18 minutes or until bottoms of cookies are light golden brown. *Do not overbake.* Cool 2 minutes on baking sheet. Roll in confectioners' sugar while warm. Remove cookies to foil to cool completely. Reroll in confectioners' sugar prior to serving.

Makes about 4 dozen cookies

Hershey's Milk Chocolate Chip Giant Cookie

BUTTERSCOTCH COOKIES WITH BURNT BUTTER ICING

½ cup butter, softened
1½ cups packed brown sugar
2 eggs
1 teaspoon vanilla
2½ cups flour
1 teaspoon baking soda
½ teaspoon salt
1 cup dairy sour cream
1 cup finely chopped walnuts
Burnt Butter Icing (recipe follows)

Beat butter and brown sugar until light and fluffy. Blend in eggs and vanilla; mix well. Add combined dry ingredients alternately with sour cream, mixing well after each addition. Stir in nuts. Chill 4 hours or overnight. Drop rounded teaspoonfuls of dough, 3 inches apart, onto well buttered cookie sheet. Bake at 400°F for 8 to 10 minutes or until lightly browned. Cool. Frost with Burnt Butter Icing.   *Makes 5 dozen cookies*

Burnt Butter Icing: Melt 6 tablespoons butter in small saucepan over medium heat; continue heating until golden brown. Cool. Blend in 2 cups sifted powdered sugar, 2 tablespoons hot water and 1 teaspoon vanilla. Add enough additional hot water, a little at a time, until spreading consistency is reached.

Favorite recipe from **Wisconsin Milk Marketing Board**

PEANUT BUTTER OATMEAL TREATS

1¾ cups all-purpose flour
1 teaspoon baking soda
½ teaspoon salt
½ cup butter or margarine, softened
½ cup SMUCKER'S® Creamy Natural Peanut Butter or LAURA SCUDDER'S® Smooth Old-Fashioned Peanut Butter
1 cup sugar
1 cup firmly packed light brown sugar
2 eggs
¼ cup milk
1 teaspoon vanilla
2½ cups uncooked oats
1 cup semi-sweet chocolate chips

Combine flour, baking soda and salt; set aside. In large mixing bowl, combine butter, peanut butter, sugar and brown sugar. Beat until light and creamy. Beat in eggs, milk and vanilla. Stir in flour mixture, oats and chocolate chips. Drop dough by rounded teaspoonfuls about 3 inches apart onto ungreased cookie sheets. Bake at 350°F for 15 minutes or until lightly browned.   *Makes 3½ dozen cookies*

COCOA SNICKERDOODLES

1 cup butter, softened
¾ cup packed brown sugar
¾ cup plus 2 tablespoons granulated
    sugar, divided
2 eggs
2 cups uncooked rolled oats
1½ cups all-purpose flour
¼ cup plus 2 tablespoons unsweetened
    cocoa powder, divided
1 teaspoon baking soda
2 tablespoons ground cinnamon

Preheat oven to 375°F. Lightly grease cookie sheets or line with parchment paper.

Beat butter, brown sugar and ¾ cup granulated sugar in large bowl until light and fluffy. Add eggs; mix well. Combine oats, flour, ¼ cup cocoa and baking soda in medium bowl. Stir into butter mixture until blended.

Mix remaining 2 tablespoons granulated sugar, remaining 2 tablespoons cocoa and cinnamon in small bowl. Drop dough by rounded teaspoonfuls into cinnamon mixture; toss to coat. Place 2 inches apart on prepared cookie sheets.

Bake 8 to 10 minutes or until firm in center. *Do not overbake.* Remove to wire racks to cool.
Makes about 4½ dozen cookies

WHITE CHOCOLATE CHIP & MACADAMIA COOKIES

2 squares (1 ounce each) unsweetened
    chocolate
½ cup butter, softened
1 cup packed light brown sugar
1 egg
1 teaspoon vanilla
1¼ cups all-purpose flour
½ teaspoon baking soda
1 cup (6 ounces) white chocolate chips
¾ cup macadamia nuts, chopped

Preheat oven to 350°F. Lightly grease cookie sheets or line with parchment paper. Melt unsweetened chocolate in top of double boiler over hot, not boiling, water. Remove from heat; cool. Cream butter, melted chocolate and sugar in large bowl until blended. Add egg and vanilla; beat until light. Blend in flour, baking soda, chocolate chips and macadamia nuts. Drop dough by rounded teaspoonfuls 2 inches apart onto prepared cookie sheets. Bake 10 to 12 minutes or until firm. *Do not overbake.* Remove to wire racks to cool.
Makes about 4 dozen cookies

LEMONY BUTTER COOKIES

½ cup butter, softened
½ cup sugar
1 egg
1½ cups all-purpose flour
1 teaspoon grated lemon peel
2 tablespoons fresh lemon juice
½ teaspoon baking powder
⅛ teaspoon salt
    Additional sugar

Beat butter and sugar in large bowl with electric mixer until creamy. Beat in egg until light and fluffy. Mix in flour, lemon peel and juice, baking powder and salt. Cover; refrigerate about 2 hours or until firm.

Preheat oven to 350°F. Roll out dough, a small portion at a time, on well-floured surface to ¼-inch thickness. (Keep remaining dough in refrigerator.) Cut with 3-inch round cookie cutter. Transfer to ungreased cookie sheets. Sprinkle with sugar.

Bake 8 to 10 minutes or until lightly browned on edges. Cool 1 minute on cookie sheets. Remove to wire racks; cool completely. Store in airtight container.

Makes about 2½ dozen cookies

CHOCOLATE CHIPS COOKIES WITH MACADAMIA NUTS

⅔ cup butter or margarine, softened
½ cup packed light brown sugar
½ cup granulated sugar
1 teaspoon vanilla extract
1 egg
1 cup all-purpose flour
⅓ cup HERSHEY'S Cocoa
½ teaspoon baking soda
½ teaspoon salt
2 cups (12-ounce package) HERSHEY'S
    Semi-Sweet Chocolate Chips
¾ cup (3½-ounce jar) macadamia nuts,
    coarsely chopped

1. Beat butter, brown sugar, granulated sugar and vanilla in large bowl until creamy. Add egg; blend well.

2. Stir together flour, cocoa, baking soda and salt; gradually add to butter mixture, blending well. Stir in chocolate chips and nuts. Cover; refrigerate 1 to 2 hours.

3. Heat oven to 350°F. Very lightly grease cookie sheet. Using ice cream scoop or ¼ cup measuring cup, drop dough onto prepared cookie sheet; flatten slightly.

4. Bake 10 to 12 minutes. (Do not overbake; cookies will be soft. They will puff during baking and flatten upon cooling.) Cool slightly; remove from cookie sheet to wire rack. Cool completely.

Makes about 1 dozen cookies

Lemony Butter Cookie

SWEDISH SANDWICH COOKIES (SYLTKAKOR)

1 cup butter, softened
½ cup plus 2 tablespoons sugar, divided
1 large egg yolk
1 large egg, separated
2 to 2¼ cups all-purpose flour
3 tablespoons ground almonds
3 tablespoons red currant or strawberry
    jelly

1. Grease and flour cookie sheets; set aside. Beat butter and ½ cup sugar in large bowl with electric mixer at medium speed until light and fluffy. Beat in egg yolks.

2. Gradually add 1½ cups flour; beat at low speed until well blended. Stir in additional flour with spoon to form stiff dough. Form dough into 2 discs; wrap in plastic wrap and refrigerate until firm, at least 2 hours.

3. Preheat oven to 375°F. Unwrap 1 disc and place on lightly floured surface. Roll out dough with lightly floured rolling pin to ⅛-inch thickness.

4. Cut dough with floured 2¼-inch *round* cookie cutter. Place cookies 1½ to 2 inches apart on prepared cookie sheets. Gently knead dough trimmings together; reroll and cut out more cookies.

5. Repeat step 3 with second disc.

6. Cut dough with floured 2¼-inch *scalloped* cookie cutter. Cut 1-inch centers out of scalloped cookies. Place cookies 1½ to 2 inches apart on prepared cookie sheets. (Cut equal numbers of round and scalloped cookies.)

7. Beat egg white in small cup with wire whisk. Combine almonds and remaining 2 tablespoons sugar in small bowl. Brush each scalloped cookie with egg white; sprinkle with sugar mixture. Bake cookies 8 to 10 minutes or until firm and light golden brown. Remove cookies to wire racks; cool completely.

8. To assemble cookies, spread about ½ teaspoon currant jelly over flat side of round cookies; top with flat side of scalloped cookies to form sandwich.

9. Store tightly covered at room temperature or freeze up to 3 months.

Makes 1½ dozen sandwich cookies

To reduce the risk of overprocessing when grinding nuts in a food processor or blender, add a small amount of the flour or sugar from the recipe.

Swedish Sandwich Cookies (Syltkakor)

CHOCOLATE SENSATIONS

CHOCOLATE CRACKLETOPS

2 cups all-purpose flour
2 teaspoons baking powder
2 cups granulated sugar
½ cup (1 stick) butter or margarine
4 squares (1 ounce each) unsweetened baking chocolate, chopped
4 large eggs, lightly beaten
2 teaspoons vanilla extract
1¾ cups "M&M's"® Chocolate Mini Baking Bits
   Additional granulated sugar

Combine flour and baking powder; set aside. In 2-quart saucepan over medium heat combine 2 cups sugar, butter and chocolate, stirring until butter and chocolate are melted; remove from heat. Gradually stir in eggs and vanilla. Stir in flour mixture until well blended. Chill mixture 1 hour. Stir in "M&M's"® Chocolate Mini Baking Bits; chill mixture an additional 1 hour.

Preheat oven to 350°F. Line cookie sheets with foil. With sugar-dusted hands, roll dough into 1-inch balls; roll balls in additional granulated sugar. Place about 2 inches apart onto prepared cookie sheets. Bake 10 to 12 minutes. *Do not overbake.* Cool completely on wire racks. Store in tightly covered container.   *Makes about 5 dozen cookies*

Chocolate Crackletops

RASPBERRY–FILLED CHOCOLATE RAVIOLI

1 cup butter, softened
½ cup granulated sugar
2 squares (1 ounce each) bittersweet or semisweet chocolate, melted and cooled
1 egg
1 teaspoon vanilla
½ teaspoon chocolate extract
¼ teaspoon baking soda
    Dash salt
2½ cups all-purpose flour
1 to 1¼ cups seedless raspberry jam
    Powdered sugar

Mix butter and granulated sugar in large bowl until blended. Add melted chocolate, egg, vanilla, chocolate extract, baking soda and salt; beat until light. Blend in flour to make stiff dough. Divide dough in half. Cover; refrigerate until firm.

Preheat oven to 350°F. Lightly grease cookie sheets or line with parchment paper. Roll out dough, half at a time, ⅛ inch thick between two sheets of plastic wrap. Remove top sheet of plastic. (If dough gets too soft and sticks to plastic, refrigerate until firm.) Cut dough into 1½-inch squares. Place half of the squares, 2 inches apart, on prepared cookie sheets. Place about ½ teaspoon jam on center of each square; top with another square. Using fork, press edges of squares together to seal, then pierce center of each square. Bake 10 minutes or just until edges are browned. Remove to wire racks to cool. Dust lightly with powdered sugar.

Makes about 6 dozen cookies

WHITE CHOCOLATE BIGGIES

1½ cups butter, softened
1 cup granulated sugar
¾ cup packed light brown sugar
2 eggs
2 teaspoons vanilla
2½ cups all-purpose flour
⅔ cup unsweetened cocoa powder
1 teaspoon baking soda
½ teaspoon salt
1 package (10 ounces) large white chocolate chips
¾ cup pecan halves, coarsely chopped
½ cup golden raisins

Preheat oven to 350°F. Lightly grease cookie sheets or line with parchment paper.

Beat butter, sugars, eggs and vanilla in large bowl until light and fluffy. Combine flour, cocoa, baking soda and salt in medium bowl; blend into butter mixture until smooth. Stir in white chocolate chips, pecans and raisins.

Scoop out about ⅓ cup dough for each cookie Place on prepared cookie sheets, spacing about 4 inches apart. Press each cookie to flatten slightly.

Bake 12 to 14 minutes or until firm in center. Cool 5 minutes on cookie sheets; remove to wire racks to cool completely.

Makes about 2 dozen cookie

Raspberry-Filled Chocolate Ravic

CHOCOLATE THUMBPRINT COOKIES

½ cup (1 stick) butter or margarine, softened
⅔ cup sugar
1 egg, separated
2 tablespoons milk
1 teaspoon vanilla extract
1 cup all-purpose flour
⅓ cup HERSHEY'S Cocoa
¼ teaspoon salt
1 cup chopped nuts
  Vanilla Filling (recipe follows)
26 HERSHEY'S KISSES Milk Chocolates, HERSHEY'S HUGS Chocolates or pecan halves or candied cherry halves

1. Beat butter, sugar, egg yolk, milk and vanilla in medium bowl until light and fluffy. Stir together flour, cocoa and salt; gradually add to butter mixture, beating until blended. Refrigerate dough at least 1 hour or until firm enough to handle.

2. Heat oven to 350°F. Lightly grease cookie sheet. Shape dough into 1-inch balls. With fork, beat egg white slightly. Dip each ball into egg white; roll in nuts. Place on prepared cookie sheet. Press thumb gently in center of each cookie.

3. Bake cookies 10 to 12 minutes or until set. Meanwhile, prepare Vanilla Filling. Remove wrappers from chocolate pieces. Remove cookies from cookie sheet to wire rack; cool 5 minutes. Spoon about ¼ teaspoon prepared filling into each thumbprint. Gently press chocolate piece onto top of each cookie. Cool completely.   *Makes about 2 dozen cookies*

VANILLA FILLING

½ cup powdered sugar
1 tablespoon butter or margarine, softened
2 teaspoons milk
¼ teaspoon vanilla extract

Combine powdered sugar, butter, milk and vanilla; beat until smooth.

CHOCOLATE PLATTER COOKIES

1 cup unsalted butter, softened
1 cup packed light brown sugar
½ cup granulated sugar
2 eggs
2⅓ cups all-purpose flour
1 teaspoon baking soda
½ teaspoon salt
1 package (12 ounces) semisweet chocolate chunks
2 cups chopped pecans

Preheat oven to 375°F. Lightly grease cookie sheets or line with parchment paper. Cream butter with sugars until smooth. Add eggs; beat until fluffy. Combine flour, baking soda and salt in small bowl. Add to creamed mixture, mixing until dough is stiff. Stir in chocolate chunks and pecans. Scoop out about ⅓ cupful of dough for each cookie. Place on prepared cookie sheets, spacing 4 inches apart. Using back of fork, flatten each cookie to about ½ inch thick. Bake 15 minutes or until light golden. Remove to wire racks to cool.   *Makes about 16 cookies*

COFFEE CHIP DROPS

1¼ cups firmly packed light brown sugar
¾ Butter Flavor* CRISCO® Stick or ¾ cup Butter Flavor CRISCO® all-vegetable shortening
2 tablespoons cold coffee
1 teaspoon vanilla extract
1 egg
1¾ cups all-purpose flour
1 tablespoon finely ground French roast or espresso coffee beans
1 teaspoon salt
¾ teaspoon baking soda
½ cup semisweet chocolate chips
½ cup milk chocolate chips
½ cup coarsely chopped walnuts
30 to 40 chocolate kiss candies, unwrapped

Butter Flavor Crisco is artificially flavored.

1. Heat oven to 375°F. Place sheets of foil on countertop for cooling cookies.

2. Place brown sugar, ¾ cup shortening, coffee and vanilla in large bowl. Beat at medium speed of electric mixer until well blended. Add egg; beat well.

3. Combine flour, ground coffee, salt and baking soda. Add to shortening mixture; beat at low speed just until blended. Stir in chocolate chips and walnuts.

4. Drop dough by rounded tablespoonfuls 2 inches apart onto ungreased baking sheets.

5. Bake one baking sheet at a time at 375°F for 8 to 10 minutes or until cookies are lightly browned and just set. *Do not overbake.* Place 1 candy in center of each cookie. Cool 2 minutes on baking sheet. Remove cookies to foil to cool completely.

Makes about 3 dozen cookies

CHOCOLATE CHERRY COOKIES

½ cup butter, softened
½ cup sugar
1 egg
2 squares (1 ounce each) unsweetened chocolate, melted and cooled
2 cups cake flour
1 teaspoon vanilla
¼ teaspoon salt
Maraschino cherries, well drained (about 48)
1 cup (6 ounces) semisweet or milk chocolate chips

Beat butter and sugar in large bowl until light. Add egg and melted chocolate; beat until fluffy. Stir in cake flour, vanilla and salt until well blended. Cover; refrigerate until firm, about 1 hour.

Preheat oven to 400°F. Lightly grease cookie sheets or line with parchment paper. Shape dough into 1-inch balls. Place 2 inches apart on prepared cookie sheets. With knuckle of finger, make deep indentation in center of each ball. Place cherry into each indentation. Bake 8 minutes or just until set. Meanwhile, melt chocolate chips in small bowl over hot water. Stir until melted. Remove cookies to wire racks. Drizzle melted chocolate over tops of cookies while still warm. Refrigerate until chocolate is set.

Makes about 4 dozen cookies

DOUBLE CHOCOLATE CHUNK COOKIES

2 squares (1 ounce each) unsweetened chocolate
3 eggs
1 cup vegetable oil
¾ cup packed brown sugar
1 teaspoon baking powder
1 teaspoon vanilla
¼ teaspoon baking soda
¼ teaspoon salt
2⅓ cups all-purpose flour
1 package (12 ounces) semisweet chocolate chunks

Preheat oven to 350°F. Lightly grease cookie sheets or line with parchment paper. Melt unsweetened chocolate in top of double boiler over hot, not boiling, water. Remove from heat; cool. Beat eggs in large bowl until foamy. Add oil and sugar; continue beating until light and frothy. Blend in baking powder, vanilla, baking soda, salt and melted chocolate. Mix in flour until smooth. Stir in chocolate chunks. Shape dough into walnut-sized balls. Place 2 inches apart on prepared cookie sheets. Bake 10 to 12 minutes or until firm in center. *Do not overbake.* Remove to wire racks to cool.

Makes about 4½ dozen cookies

White Chocolate Chunk Cookies: Substitute one package (12 ounces) white chocolate chunks or two white chocolate candy bars (5 to 6 ounces each), cut into chunks, for the semisweet chocolate chunks.

ALMOND CHOCOLATE KISS COOKIES

½ cup sugar
½ cup margarine or butter, softened
¼ cup egg substitute
1 teaspoon almond extract
1⅓ cups all-purpose flour
1 teaspoon baking soda
½ cup PLANTERS® Slivered Almonds, toasted and finely chopped
24 chocolate candy kisses

1. Beat sugar and margarine in large bowl with mixer at medium speed until creamy. Blend in egg substitute and almond extract.

2. Mix flour and baking soda in small bowl; stir into egg mixture.

3. Shape dough into 1-inch balls; roll in toasted almonds. Place 2 inches apart on ungreased baking sheets. Bake in preheated 350°F oven for 7 to 9 minutes or until lightly golden; remove from oven. Immediately top each cookie with a candy kiss, pressing lightly into center of cookie.

4. Remove from sheets. Cool completely on wire racks. Store in airtight container.

Makes 2 dozen cookies

Preparation Time: 25 minutes
Cook Time: 7 minutes
Total Time: 32 minutes

White Chocolate Chunk Cookies

THE YALE
SHAKESPEARE

KING HENRY
THE FIFTH

Edited by
ROBERT D. FRENCH

YALE UNIVERSITY
PRESS

FUDGEY GERMAN CHOCOLATE SANDWICH COOKIES

1¾ cups all-purpose flour
1½ cups sugar
¾ cup (1½ sticks) butter or margarine, softened
⅔ cup HERSHEY₂S Cocoa or HERSHEY₂S Dutch Processed Cocoa
¾ teaspoon baking soda
¼ teaspoon salt
2 eggs
2 tablespoons milk
1 teaspoon vanilla extract
½ cup finely chopped pecans
Coconut and Pecan Filling (recipe follows)

1. Heat oven to 350°F. In large bowl, combine flour, sugar, butter, cocoa, baking soda, salt, eggs, milk and vanilla. Beat at medium speed of electric mixer until blended (batter will be stiff). Stir in pecans.

2. Form batter into 1¼-inch balls. Place on ungreased cookie sheet; flatten slightly.

3. Bake 9 to 11 minutes or until almost set. Cool slightly; remove from cookie sheet to wire rack. Cool completely. Spread about 1 heaping tablespoon Coconut and Pecan Filling onto bottom of one cookie. Top with second cookie to make sandwich. Serve warm or at room temperature.

Makes about 17 sandwich cookies

Prep Time: 25 minutes
Bake Time: 9 minutes
Cool Time: 35 minutes

COCONUT AND PECAN FILLING

½ cup (1 stick) butter or margarine
½ cup packed light brown sugar
¼ cup light corn syrup
1 cup MOUNDS® Sweetened Coconut Flakes, toasted*
1 cup finely chopped pecans
1 teaspoon vanilla extract

*To toast coconut: Heat oven to 350°F. Spread coconut in even layer on baking sheet. Bake 6 to 8 minutes, stirring occasionally, until golden.

Melt butter in medium saucepan; add brown sugar and corn syrup. Stir constantly, until thick and bubbly. Remove from heat; stir in coconut, pecans and vanilla. Use warm.

Makes about 2 cups filling

Grease cookie sheets only if directed to do so in the recipe. Some cookie doughs are high enough in fat that they will not stick to the sheet.

Fudgey German Chocolate Sandwich Cookie

SIMPLY ELEGANT

VIENNESE MERINGUE BARS

1 cup butter, softened
1¼ cups sugar, divided
2 egg yolks
¼ teaspoon salt
2¼ cups all-purpose flour
1 cup seedless raspberry jam
1½ cups mini semisweet chocolate chips
3 egg whites
½ cup slivered almonds, toasted

Preheat oven to 350°F. Beat butter and ½ cup sugar in large bowl with electric mixer at medium speed until light and fluffy. Beat in egg yolks and salt. Gradually add flour. Beat at low speed until well blended.

With buttered fingers, pat dough evenly into ungreased 15×10-inch jelly-roll pan. Bake 22 to 25 minutes or until light golden brown. Remove from oven; immediately spread jam over crust. Sprinkle evenly with chocolate chips.

For meringue topping, beat egg whites in clean large bowl with electric mixer on high speed until foamy. Gradually beat in remaining ¾ cup sugar until stiff peaks form. Gently stir in almonds with rubber spatula.

Spoon meringue over chocolate mixture; spread evenly with small spatula. Bake 20 to 25 minutes or until golden brown. Cool completely on wire rack. Cut into bars.   *Makes 28 bars*

Viennese Meringue Bar

CHOCOLATE ALMOND BISCOTTI

  3 cups all-purpose flour
½ cup unsweetened cocoa
  2 teaspoons baking powder
½ teaspoon salt
  1 cup granulated sugar
⅔ cup FLEISCHMANN'S® Original
    Margarine, softened
¾ cup EGG BEATERS® Healthy Real Egg
    Product
  1 teaspoon almond extract
½ cup whole blanched almonds, toasted
    and coarsely chopped
    Powdered Sugar Glaze (recipe follows)

In medium bowl, combine flour, cocoa, baking powder and salt; set aside.

In large bowl, with electric mixer at medium speed, beat granulated sugar and margarine for 2 minutes or until creamy. Add Egg Beaters® and almond extract; beat well. With electric mixer at low speed, gradually add flour mixture, beating just until blended; stir in almonds.

On lightly greased baking sheet, form dough into two (12×2½-inch) logs. Bake at 350°F for 25 to 30 minutes or until toothpick inserted in centers comes out clean. Remove from sheet; cool on wire racks 15 minutes.

Using serrated knife, slice each log diagonally into 12 (1-inch-thick) slices; place, cut sides up, on same baking sheet. Bake at 350°F for 12 to 15 minutes on each side or until cookies are crisp and edges are browned. Remove from sheet; cool completely on wire rack. Drizzle tops with Powdered Sugar Glaze.

Makes 2 dozen cookies

Powdered Sugar Glaze: In small bowl, combine 1 cup powdered sugar and 5 to 6 teaspoons water until smooth.

Prep Time: 25 minutes
Cook Time: 45 minutes

Biscotti are traditional Italian cookies that are baked twice to produce their characteristic crunchy texture. They are ideal for dipping in coffee, tea or dessert wine.

Chocolate Almond Biscotti

TOFFEE SPATTERED SUGAR STARS

1¼ cups granulated sugar
 1 Butter Flavor* CRISCO® stick or 1 cup Butter Flavor CRISCO® all-vegetable shortening
 2 eggs
 ¼ cup light corn syrup or regular pancake syrup
 1 tablespoon vanilla extract
 3 cups all-purpose flour (plus 4 tablespoons), divided
 ¾ teaspoon baking powder
 ½ teaspoon baking soda
 ½ teaspoon salt
 1 package (6 ounces) milk chocolate English toffee chips, divided

Butter Flavor Crisco is artificially flavored.

1. Place sugar and 1 cup shortening in large bowl. Beat at medium speed of electric mixer until well blended. Add eggs, syrup and vanilla; beat until well blended and fluffy.

2. Combine 3 cups flour, baking powder, baking soda and salt. Add gradually to shortening mixture, beating at low speed until well blended.

3. Divide dough into 4 equal pieces; shape each into disk. Wrap with plastic wrap. Refrigerate 1 hour or until firm.

4. Heat oven to 375°F. Place sheets of foil on countertop for cooling cookies.

5. Sprinkle about 1 tablespoon flour on large sheet of waxed paper. Place disk of dough on floured paper; flatten slightly with hands. Turn dough over; cover with another large sheet of waxed paper. Roll dough to ¼-inch thickness. Remove top sheet of waxed paper. Sprinkle about ¼ of toffee chips over dough. Roll lightly into dough. Cut out with floured star or round cookie cutter. Place 2 inches apart on ungreased baking sheet. Repeat with remaining dough and toffee chips.

6. Bake one baking sheet at a time at 375°F for 5 to 7 minutes or until cookies are lightly browned around edges. *Do not overbake.* Cool 2 minutes on baking sheet. Remove cookies to foil to cool completely.

Makes about 3½ dozen cookies.

When reusing cookie sheets for several batches of cookies, cool the sheets completely before placing more dough on them. Dough will soften and begin to spread if placed on a hot cookie sheet.

From top to bottom: Pecan Cookies (page 10) and Toffee Spattered Sugar Stars

PEEK–A–BOO APRICOT COOKIES

4 ounces bittersweet chocolate candy bar, broken into pieces
3 cups all-purpose flour
½ teaspoon baking soda
½ teaspoon salt
⅔ cup butter, softened
¾ cup sugar
2 large eggs
2 teaspoons vanilla
Apricot preserves

1. Melt chocolate in small bowl set in bowl of very hot water, stirring twice. Combine flour, baking soda and salt in medium bowl.

2. Beat butter and sugar in large bowl with electric mixer at medium speed until light and fluffy. Beat in eggs, 1 at a time, beating well after each addition. Beat in vanilla and chocolate. Beat in flour mixture at low speed until well blended.

3. Divide dough into 2 rounds; flatten into discs. Wrap in plastic wrap; refrigerate 2 hours or until firm.

4. Preheat oven to 350°F.

5. Roll out dough on lightly floured surface to ¼- to ⅛-inch thickness. Cut out rounds with 2½-inch cutter. Cut 1-inch centers out of half the rounds. Reserve scraps. Place rounds on ungreased cookie sheets. Repeat rolling and cutting with remaining scraps of dough.

6. Bake cookies 9 to 10 minutes or until set. Let cookies stand on cookie sheets 2 minutes. Remove cookies with spatula to wire rack; cool completely.

7. To assemble cookies, spread about 1½ teaspoons preserves over flat side of cookie circles; top with cut-out cookies to form a sandwich.

8. Store tightly covered at room temperature. These cookies do not freeze well.
Makes about 1½ dozen sandwich cookies

HERSHEY®'S MINT CHOCOLATE COOKIES

¾ cup (1½ sticks) butter or margarine, softened
1 cup sugar
1 egg
1 teaspoon vanilla extract
1½ cups all-purpose flour
½ teaspoon baking soda
¼ teaspoon salt
1⅔ cups (10-ounce package) HERSHEY®'S Mint Chocolate Chips

1. Heat oven to 350°F.

2. Beat beat butter and sugar in large bowl until light and fluffy. Add egg and vanilla; beat well. Stir together flour, baking soda and salt; gradually blend into butter mixture. Stir in chocolate chips. Drop by rounded teaspoonfuls onto ungreased cookie sheet.

3. Bake 8 to 9 minutes or just until lightly browned. Cool slightly; remove from cookie sheet to wire rack. Cool completely.
Makes about 2½ dozen cookies

Peek-a-Boo Apricot Cookie

ORANGE–CARDAMOM THINS

1¼ cups granulated sugar
  1 Butter Flavor* CRISCO® Stick or 1 cup
      Butter Flavor CRISCO® all-vegetable
      shortening plus additional for
      greasing
  1 egg
¼ cup light corn syrup or regular pancake
      syrup
  1 teaspoon vanilla extract
  1 tablespoon grated orange peel
½ teaspoon orange extract
  3 cups all-purpose flour
1¼ teaspoons cardamom
¾ teaspoon baking powder
½ teaspoon baking soda
½ teaspoon salt
½ teaspoon cinnamon

Butter Flavor Crisco is artificially flavored.

1. Place sugar and 1 cup shortening in large bowl. Beat at medium speed of electric mixer until well blended. Add egg, syrup, vanilla, orange peel and orange extract; beat until well blended and fluffy.

2. Combine flour, cardamom, baking powder, baking soda, salt and cinnamon. Add gradually to shortening mixture, beating at low speed until well blended.

3. Divide dough in half. Roll each half into 12-inch-long log. Wrap with plastic wrap. Refrigerate for 4 hours or until firm.

4. Heat oven to 375°F. Grease baking sheets. Place sheets of foil on countertop for cooling cookies.

5. Cut rolls into ¼-inch-thick slices. Place 1 inch apart on prepared baking sheets.

6. Bake one baking sheet at a time at 375°F for 7 to 9 minutes or until bottoms of cookies are lightly browned. *Do not overbake.* Cool 2 minutes on baking sheet. Remove cookies to foil to cool completely.

Makes about 8 dozen cookies

ALMOND LACE COOKIES

¼ cup butter, softened
½ cup sugar
½ cup BLUE DIAMOND® Blanched
      Almond Paste
¼ cup all-purpose flour
¼ teaspoon salt
½ teaspoon almond extract
  2 tablespoons milk
  2 teaspoons grated orange peel

Cream butter and sugar. Beat in almond paste. Add remaining ingredients. Mix well. Drop rounded teaspoonfuls onto cookie sheet, 3 inches apart. (Cookies will spread.) Bake at 350°F for 8 to 10 minutes or until edges are lightly browned. Cool 3 to 4 minutes on cookie sheet; remove and cool on wire rack.

Makes 1½ dozen cookies

DOUBLE–DIPPED HAZELNUT CRISPS

¾ **cup semisweet chocolate chips**
1¼ **cups all-purpose flour**
¾ **cup powdered sugar**
⅔ **cup whole hazelnuts, toasted, skinned and ground***
¼ **teaspoon instant espresso powder**
 Dash salt
½ **cup butter, softened**
2 **teaspoons vanilla**
4 **squares (1 ounce each) bittersweet or semisweet chocolate**
2 **teaspoons shortening, divided**
4 **ounces white chocolate**

To grind hazelnuts, place in food processor or blender. Process until thoroughly ground with a dry, not pasty, texture.

Preheat oven to 350°F. Lightly grease cookie sheets or line with parchment paper. Melt chocolate chips in top of double boiler over hot, not boiling, water. Remove from heat; cool. Blend flour, sugar, hazelnuts, espresso powder and salt in large bowl. Blend in butter, melted chocolate and vanilla until dough is stiff but smooth. (If dough is too soft to handle, cover and refrigerate until firm.)

Roll out dough, ¼ at a time, to ⅛-inch thickness on lightly floured surface. Cut out with 2-inch scalloped round cutters. Place 2 inches apart on prepared cookie sheets. Bake 8 minutes or until not quite firm. (Cookies should not brown. They will puff up during baking and then fall again.) Remove to wire racks to cool.

Place bittersweet chocolate and 1 teaspoon shortening in small bowl. Place bowl over hot water; stir until chocolate is melted and smooth. Dip cookies, 1 at a time, halfway into bittersweet chocolate. Place on waxed paper; refrigerate until chocolate is set. Repeat melting process with white chocolate. Dip other halves of cookies into white chocolate; refrigerate until set. Store cookies in airtight container in cool place. (If cookies are frozen, chocolate might discolor.)

Makes about 4 dozen cookies

To melt chocolate in a microwave oven, place 2 unwrapped squares or 1 cup chips in a microwavable bowl. Microwave at HIGH for 1 to 1½ minutes, stirring after 1 minute. Be sure to stir chocolate, since it may retain its original shape even when melted.

ORANGE & CHOCOLATE RIBBON COOKIES

1 cup (2 sticks) butter, softened
½ cup sugar
3 egg yolks
2 teaspoons grated orange peel
1 teaspoon orange extract
2¼ cups all-purpose flour, divided
3 tablespoons unsweetened cocoa powder
1 teaspoon vanilla
1 teaspoon chocolate extract

Beat butter, sugar and egg yolks in large bowl until light and fluffy. Remove half of mixture; place in another bowl. Add orange peel, orange extract and 1¼ cups of the flour to one bowl; mix until blended and smooth. Shape into a ball. Add cocoa, vanilla and chocolate extract to remaining mixture; beat until smooth. Stir in remaining 1 cup flour; mix until blended and smooth. Shape into a ball. Cover dough; refrigerate 10 minutes.

Roll out each dough separately on lightly floured surface to 12×4-inch rectangle. Pat edges of dough to straighten; use rolling pin to level off thickness. Place one dough on top of the other. Using sharp knife, make lengthwise cut through center of doughs. Lift half of dough onto other to make long, 4-layer strip of dough. With hands, press dough strips together. Wrap in plastic wrap; refrigerate at least 1 hour or up to 3 days.

Preheat oven to 350°F. Grease cookie sheets. Cut dough crosswise into ¼-inch-thick slices; place 2 inches apart on prepared cookie sheets. Bake 10 to 12 minutes or until very lightly browned. Remove to wire racks to cool. *Makes about 5 dozen cookies*

MARVELOUS MACAROONS

1 can (8 ounces) DOLE® Crushed Pineapple
1 can (14 ounces) sweetened condensed milk
1 package (7 ounces) flaked coconut
½ cup margarine, melted
½ cup chopped almonds, toasted
1 teaspoon grated lemon peel
¼ teaspoon almond extract
1 cup all-purpose flour
1 teaspoon baking powder

• Preheat oven to 350°F. Drain pineapple well, pressing out excess juice with back of spoon. In large bowl, combine drained pineapple, milk, coconut, margarine, almonds, lemon peel and almond extract.

• In small bowl, combine flour and baking powder. Beat into pineapple mixture until blended. Drop heaping tablespoonfuls of dough 1 inch apart onto greased cookie sheets.

• Bake 13 to 15 minutes or until lightly browned. Garnish with whole almonds, if desired. Cool on wire racks. Store in covered container in refrigerator.
Makes about 3½ dozen cookies

Marvelous Macaroons

CHOCOLATE
SURPRISE COOKIES

2¾ cups all-purpose flour
¾ cup unsweetened cocoa powder
½ teaspoon baking powder
½ teaspoon baking soda
1 cup (2 sticks) butter, softened
1½ cups packed light brown sugar
½ cup plus 1 tablespoon granulated sugar,
    divided
2 eggs
1 teaspoon vanilla
1 cup chopped pecans, divided
1 package (9 ounces) caramels coated in
    milk chocolate
3 squares (1 ounce each) white chocolate,
    coarsely chopped

Preheat oven to 375°F. Combine flour, cocoa, baking powder and baking soda in medium bowl; set aside.

Beat butter, brown sugar and ½ cup granulated sugar with electric mixer at medium speed until light and fluffy; beat in eggs and vanilla. Gradually add flour mixture and ½ cup pecans; beat well. Cover dough; refrigerate 15 minutes or until firm enough to roll into balls.

Place remaining ½ cup pecans and 1 tablespoon sugar in shallow dish. Roll tablespoonful of dough around 1 caramel candy, covering completely; press one side into nut mixture. Place, nut side up, on ungreased cookie sheet. Repeat with additional dough and candies, placing 3 inches apart.

Bake 10 to 12 minutes or until set and slightly cracked. Let stand on cookie sheet 2 minutes. Transfer cookies to wire rack; cool completely.

Place white chocolate pieces in small resealable plastic food storage bag; seal bag. Microwave at MEDIUM (50% power) 2 minutes. Turn bag over; microwave 2 to 3 minutes or until melted. Knead bag until chocolate is smooth. Cut off tiny corner of bag; drizzle chocolate onto cookies. Let stand about 30 minutes or until chocolate is set.

Makes about 3½ dozen cookies

Cooling cookies for a minute or two on cookie sheets allows them to set. Otherwise they may be too tender to move right out of the oven.

Chocolate Surprise Cookies

MORAVIAN SPICE CRISPS

⅓ cup shortening
⅓ cup packed brown sugar
¼ cup unsulfured molasses
¼ cup dark corn syrup
1¾ to 2 cups all-purpose flour
2 teaspoons ground ginger
1¼ teaspoons baking soda
1 teaspoon ground cinnamon
½ teaspoon ground cloves
Powdered sugar

1. Melt shortening in small saucepan over low heat. Remove from heat; stir in brown sugar, molasses and corn syrup. Set aside; cool.

2. Place 1½ cups flour, ginger, baking soda, cinnamon and cloves in large bowl; stir to combine. Beat in shortening mixture with electric mixer at medium speed. Gradually beat in additional flour until stiff dough forms.

3. Knead dough on lightly floured surface, adding more flour if too sticky. Form dough into 2 discs; wrap in plastic wrap and refrigerate 30 minutes or until firm.

4. Preheat oven to 350°F. Grease cookie sheets; set aside. Working with 1 disc at a time, roll out dough on lightly floured surface to 1/16-inch thickness.

5. Cut dough with floured 2⅜-inch scalloped cookie cutter. (If dough becomes too soft, refrigerate several minutes before continuing.) Gently press dough trimmings together; reroll and cut out more cookies. Place cookies ½ inch apart on prepared cookie sheets.

6. Bake 8 minutes or until firm and lightly browned. Remove cookies with spatula to wire racks; cool completely.

7. Place small strips of cardboard or parchment paper over cookies; dust with sifted powdered sugar. Carefully remove cardboard. *Makes about 6 dozen cookies*

GREEK LEMON–HERB COOKIES

2½ cups all-purpose flour
1 teaspoon baking soda
¼ teaspoon salt
1 cup butter, softened
1¼ cups sugar, divided
2 large eggs, separated
4 teaspoons grated lemon peel, divided
½ teaspoon dried rosemary leaves, crushed

1. Preheat oven to 375°F. Place flour, baking soda and salt in large bowl; stir to combine.

2. Beat butter and 1 cup sugar in large bowl with electric mixer at medium speed until light and fluffy. Beat in egg yolks, 3 teaspoons lemon peel and rosemary. Gradually add flour mixture. Beat at low speed until well blended.

3. Combine remaining ¼ cup sugar and 1 teaspoon lemon peel in small bowl.

4. Roll tablespoonfuls of dough into 1-inch balls; roll in sugar mixture to coat.

5. Place balls 2 inches apart on *ungreased* cookie sheets. Press balls to ¼-inch thickness using flat bottom of drinking glass.

6. Bake 10 to 12 minutes or until edges are golden brown. Remove cookies to wire racks; cool completely.

7. Store tightly covered at room temperature or freeze up to 3 months.

Makes about 4 dozen cookies

Moravian Spice Crisps

DELICIOUSLY EASY

CHOCO–COCO PECAN CRISPS

½ cup butter, softened
1 cup packed light brown sugar
1 egg
1 teaspoon vanilla
1½ cups all-purpose flour
1 cup chopped pecans
⅓ cup unsweetened cocoa
½ teaspoon baking soda
1 cup flaked coconut

Cream butter and sugar in large bowl until light and fluffy. Beat in egg and vanilla. Combine flour, pecans, cocoa and baking soda in small bowl until well blended. Add to creamed mixture, blending until stiff dough is formed. Sprinkle coconut on work surface. Divide dough into 4 parts. Shape each part into a roll about 1½ inches in diameter; roll in coconut until thickly coated. Wrap in plastic wrap; refrigerate until firm, at least 1 hour or up to 2 weeks.

Preheat oven to 350°F. Cut rolls into ⅛-inch-thick slices. Place 2 inches apart on ungreased cookie sheets. Bake 10 to 13 minutes or until firm, but not overly browned. Remove to wire racks to cool.

Makes about 6 dozen cookies

Choco-Coco Pecan Crisps

CHEWY LEMON–HONEY COOKIES

2 cups all-purpose flour
1½ teaspoons baking soda
½ cup honey
⅓ cup FLEISCHMANN'S® Original Margarine
¼ cup granulated sugar
1 tablespoon grated lemon peel
¼ cup EGG BEATERS® Healthy Real Egg Product
Lemon Glaze, optional (recipe follows)

In small bowl, combine flour and baking soda; set aside.

In large bowl, with electric mixer at medium speed, beat honey, margarine, granulated sugar and lemon peel until creamy. Add Egg Beaters®; beat until smooth. Gradually stir in flour mixture until blended.

Drop dough by rounded teaspoonfuls, 2 inches apart, onto lightly greased baking sheets. Bake at 350°F for 7 to 8 minutes or until lightly browned. Remove from sheets; cool completely on wire racks. Drizzle with Lemon Glaze if desired.

Makes 3½ dozen cookies

Lemon Glaze: In small bowl, combine 1 cup powdered sugar and 2 tablespoons lemon juice until smooth.

Prep Time: 20 minutes
Cook Time: 8 minutes

FLOURLESS PEANUT BUTTER COOKIES

1 cup peanut butter
1 cup packed light brown sugar
1 egg
24 milk chocolate candy stars or other solid milk chocolate candy

Preheat oven to 350°F. Combine peanut butter, sugar and egg in medium bowl until blended and smooth.

Shape dough into 24 balls about 1½ inches in diameter. Place 2 inches apart on ungreased cookie sheets. Press one chocolate star on top of each cookie. Bake 10 to 12 minutes or until set. Transfer to wire racks to cool completely.

Makes about 2 dozen cookies

Peanut butter and chocolate are a delightful combination in these super-easy flourless cookies.

Flourless Peanut Butter Cookies

CHEWY CHOCOLATE NO-BAKES

1 cup (6 ounces) semisweet chocolate pieces
16 large marshmallows
⅓ cup (5 tablespoons plus 1 teaspoon) margarine or butter
2 cups QUAKER® Oats (quick or old fashioned, uncooked)
1 cup (any combination of) raisins, diced dried mixed fruit, flaked coconut, miniature marshmallows or chopped nuts
1 teaspoon vanilla

In large saucepan over low heat, melt chocolate pieces, marshmallows and margarine, stirring until smooth. Remove from heat; cool slightly. Stir in remaining ingredients. Drop by rounded teaspoonfuls onto wax paper. Chill 2 to 3 hours. Let stand at room temperature about 15 minutes before serving. Store in tightly covered container in refrigerator. *Makes 3 dozen cookies*

Microwave Directions: Place chocolate pieces, marshmallows and margarine in large microwavable bowl. Microwave on HIGH 1 to 2 minutes or until mixture is melted and smooth, stirring every 30 seconds. Proceed as recipe directs.

FRUIT BURST COOKIES

1 cup margarine or butter, softened
¼ cup sugar
1 teaspoon almond extract
2 cups all-purpose flour
½ teaspoon salt
1 cup finely chopped nuts
  SMUCKER'S® Simply Fruit

Beat margarine and sugar until light and fluffy. Blend in almond extract. Combine flour and salt; add to mixture and blend well. Shape level tablespoonfuls of dough into balls; roll in nuts. Place 2 inches apart on ungreased cookie sheets; flatten slightly. Indent centers; fill with fruit spread. Bake at 400°F for 10 to 12 minutes or just until lightly browned. Cool. *Makes 2½ dozen cookies*

CHOCOLATE CANDY COOKIES

⅔ cup MIRACLE WHIP® Salad Dressing
1 two-layer devil's food cake mix
2 eggs
1 (8-ounce) package candy-coated chocolate candies

• Preheat oven to 375°F.

• Blend salad dressing, cake mix and eggs at low speed with electric mixer until moistened. Beat on medium speed 2 minutes. Stir in chocolate candies. (Dough will be stiff.)

• Drop by rounded teaspoonfuls, 2 inches apart, onto greased cookie sheets.

• Bake 9 to 11 minutes or until almost set. (Cookies will still appear soft.) Cool 1 minute remove from cookie sheets.
Makes about 4½ dozen cookies

LEMON COOKIES

⅔ cup MIRACLE WHIP® Salad Dressing
1 two-layer yellow cake mix
2 eggs
2 teaspoons grated lemon peel
⅔ cup ready-to-spread vanilla frosting
4 teaspoons lemon juice

• Preheat oven to 375°F.

• Blend salad dressing, cake mix and eggs at low speed with electric mixer until moistened. Add peel. Beat on medium speed 2 minutes. (Dough will be stiff.)

• Drop rounded teaspoonfuls of dough, 2 inches apart, onto greased cookie sheet.

• Bake 9 to 11 minutes or until lightly browned. (Cookies will still appear soft.) Cool 1 minute; remove from cookie sheet. Cool completely on wire rack.

• Stir together frosting and juice until well blended. Spread on cookies.

Makes about 4 dozen cookies

PEANUT BUTTER & JELLY COOKIES

1 package DUNCAN HINES® Peanut Butter Cookie Mix
¾ cup quick-cooking oats (not instant or old-fashioned)
1 egg
¼ cup vegetable oil
½ cup grape jelly
½ cup confectioners' sugar
2 teaspoons water

1. Preheat oven to 375°F.

2. Combine cookie mix, oats, egg and oil in large bowl. Stir until well blended. Divide dough into 4 equal portions. Shape each portion into 12-inch-long log on waxed paper. Place logs on ungreased cookie sheets. Press back of spoon down center of each log to form indentation. Bake at 375°F for 10 to 12 minutes or until light golden brown. Press back of spoon down center of each log again. Let stand 2 minutes on cookie sheets. Remove to cooling racks. Cool completely. Spoon 2 tablespoons jelly along indentation of each log.

3. Combine confectioners' sugar and water in small bowl. Stir until smooth. Drizzle over each log. Allow glaze to set. Cut each log diagonally into 12 slices with large, sharp knife. Store between layers of waxed paper in airtight container. *Makes about 48 cookies*

ORANGE PECAN REFRIGERATOR COOKIES

2⅓ cups all-purpose flour
½ teaspoon baking soda
¼ teaspoon salt
½ cup butter or margarine, softened
½ cup packed brown sugar
½ cup granulated sugar
1 egg, lightly beaten
   Grated peel of 1 SUNKIST® Orange
3 tablespoons fresh squeezed orange
   juice
¾ cup pecan pieces

In bowl, stir together flour, baking soda and salt. In large bowl, blend together butter, brown sugar and granulated sugar. Add egg, orange peel and juice; beat well. Stir in pecans. Gradually beat in flour mixture. (Dough will be stiff.) Divide mixture in half and shape each half (on long piece of waxed paper) into roll about 1¼ inches in diameter and 12 inches long. Roll up tightly in waxed paper. Chill several hours or overnight.

Cut into ¼-inch slices and arrange on lightly greased cookie sheets. Bake at 350°F for 10 to 12 minutes or until lightly browned. Cool on wire racks.   *Makes about 6 dozen cookies*

Chocolate Filled Sandwich Cookies: Cut each roll into ⅛-inch slices and bake as above. When cool, to make each sandwich cookie, spread about 1 teaspoon canned chocolate fudge frosting on bottom side of 1 cookie; cover with second cookie of same shape. Makes about 4 dozen double cookies.

FUDGY PEANUT BUTTER JIFFY COOKIES

2 cups granulated sugar
½ cup evaporated milk
½ cup (1 stick) margarine or butter
¼ cup unsweetened cocoa powder
2½ cups QUAKER® Oats (quick or old
   fashioned, uncooked)
½ cup peanut butter
½ cup raisins or chopped dates
2 teaspoons vanilla

In large saucepan, combine sugar, milk, margarine and cocoa. Bring to boil over medium heat, stirring frequently. Continue boiling 3 minutes. Remove from heat. Stir in oats, peanut butter, raisins and vanilla; mix well. Quickly drop by tablespoonfuls onto waxed paper or greased cookie sheet. Let stand until set. Store tightly covered at room temperature.   *Makes about 3 dozen cookies*

TOFFEE CREME SANDWICH COOKIES

1 jar (7 ounces) marshmallow creme
¼ cup toffee baking chips
48 (2-inch) sugar or fudge-striped
   shortbread cookies
   Red and green jimmies

. Combine marshmallow creme and toffee
hips in medium bowl until well blended.
Mixture will be stiff.)

2. Spread 1 teaspoon of marshmallow mixture on bottom of 1 cookie; top with bottom side of another cookie. Roll side of sandwich cookie in jimmies. Repeat with remaining marshmallow creme mixture, cookies and jimmies.   *Makes 2 dozen cookies*

Prep Time: 20 minutes

offee Creme Sandwich Cookies

3–MINUTE NO–BAKE COOKIES

  2 cups granulated sugar
  ½ cup 2% low-fat milk
  ½ cup (1 stick) margarine or butter
  ⅓ cup unsweetened cocoa powder
  3 cups QUAKER® Oats (quick or old
    fashioned, uncooked)

In large saucepan, combine sugar, milk, margarine and cocoa. Bring to boil over medium heat, stirring frequently. Continue boiling 3 minutes. Remove from heat. Stir in oats; mix well. Quickly drop by tablespoonfuls onto waxed paper or greased cookie sheet. Let stand until set. Store tightly covered at room temperature.

Makes about 3 dozen cookies

BANANA ENERGY BALLS

  1 extra-ripe, medium DOLE® Banana
  ¼ cup peanut butter
  ¼ cup semisweet chocolate chips
  2 tablespoons honey
 1⅓ cups natural wheat and barley cereal
  ⅓ cup finely chopped peanuts

• Mash banana with fork. Measure ½ cup.

• Combine banana, peanut butter and chocolate chips.

• Heat honey in microwave for 15 seconds or until hot. Add to banana mixture; stir 30 seconds. Add cereal; mix well. Cover; set aside for 30 minutes.

• Form balls using 1 tablespoon mixture, then roll in peanuts. Store in airtight container.

Makes 20 servings

QUICK CHOCOLATE SOFTIES

  1 package (18.25 ounces) devil's food cake
    mix
  ⅓ cup water
  ¼ cup butter, softened
  1 egg
  1 cup white chocolate baking chips
  ½ cup coarsely chopped walnuts

Preheat oven to 350°F. Grease cookie sheets. Combine cake mix, water, butter and egg in large bowl. Beat with electric mixer at low speed until moistened, scraping down side of bowl once. Increase speed to medium; beat 1 minute. (Dough will be thick.) Stir in chips and nuts; mix until well blended. Drop dough by heaping teaspoonfuls 2 inches apart onto prepared cookie sheets.

Bake 10 to 12 minutes or until set. Let cookies stand on cookie sheets 1 minute. Remove cookies to wire racks; cool completely.

Makes about 4 dozen cookies

Quick Chocolate Softie

NOT JUST FOR KIDS

KIDS' FAVORITE
JUMBO CHIPPERS

1 cup butter, softened
¾ cup granulated sugar
¾ cup packed brown sugar
2 eggs
1 teaspoon vanilla
2¼ cups all-purpose flour
1 teaspoon baking soda
¾ teaspoon salt
1 package (9 ounces) candy-coated chocolate pieces
1 cup peanut butter flavored chips

Preheat oven to 375°F. Beat butter, granulated sugar and brown sugar in large bowl until light and fluffy. Beat in eggs and vanilla. Add flour, baking soda and salt. Beat until well blended. Stir in chocolate pieces and peanut butter chips. Drop by rounded tablespoonfuls 3 inches apart onto ungreased cookie sheets. Bake 10 to 12 minutes or until edges are golden brown. Let cookies stand on cookie sheets 2 minutes. Remove cookies to wire racks; cool completely. *Makes 3 dozen cookies*

Note: For a change of pace, substitute white chocolate chips, chocolate chips, chocolate-covered raisins, toffee bits or any of your cookie monsters' favorite candy pieces for the candy-coated chocolate pieces.

Kids' Favorite Jumbo Chippers

SMUSHY COOKIES

COOKIES
1 package (20 ounces) refrigerated cookie
dough, any flavor
All-purpose flour (optional)

FILLINGS
Peanut butter, multi-colored miniature
marshmallows, assorted colored
sprinkles, chocolate-covered raisins
and caramel candy squares

1. Preheat oven to 350°F. Grease cookie sheets.

2. Remove dough from wrapper according to
package directions. Cut into 4 equal sections.
Reserve 1 section; refrigerate remaining 3
sections.

3. Roll reserved dough to ¼-inch thickness.
Sprinkle with flour to minimize sticking, if
necessary. Cut out cookies using 2½-inch
round cookie cutter. Transfer to prepared
cookie sheets. Repeat with remaining dough,
working with 1 section at a time.

4. Bake 8 to 11 minutes or until edges are light
golden brown. Remove to wire racks; cool
completely.

5. To make sandwich, spread about 1½
tablespoons peanut butter on underside of
1 cookie to within ¼ inch of edge. Sprinkle
with miniature marshmallows and candy
pieces. Top with second cookie, pressing
gently. Repeat with remaining cookies and
fillings.

6. Just before serving, place sandwiches on
paper towels. Microwave on HIGH (100%)
15 to 25 seconds or until fillings become soft.
Makes about 8 to 10 sandwich cookies

CRUNCHY CHOCOLATE CHIPSTERS

½ Butter Flavor* CRISCO® Stick or ½ cup
Butter Flavor CRISCO® all-vegetable
shortening plus additional for
greasing
½ cup firmly packed brown sugar
½ cup granulated sugar
2 tablespoons milk
1 egg
1 teaspoon vanilla extract
1¼ cups all-purpose flour
½ teaspoon baking soda
¼ teaspoon salt
2 cups crispy rice cereal
1 cup semisweet miniature chocolate
chips

Butter Flavor Crisco is artificially flavored.

1. Heat oven to 350°F. Grease cookie sheets
with shortening. Place sheets of foil on
countertop for cooling cookies.

2. Combine ½ cup shortening, brown sugar,
granulated sugar and milk in large bowl. Beat
at medium speed of electric mixer until well
blended. Beat in egg and vanilla.

3. Combine flour, baking soda and salt. Mix
into shortening mixture at low speed until
blended. Stir in cereal and chocolate chips.
Drop by level measuring tablespoonfuls
2 inches apart onto prepared baking sheets.

4. Bake at 350°F for 9 to 11 minutes or until
set. *Do not overbake.* Cool 2 minutes on baking
sheet. Remove cookies to foil to cool
completely.   *Makes about 4 dozen cookies*

Smushy Cookies

ANGEL PILLOWS

½ **Butter Flavor* CRISCO® Stick or ½ cup Butter Flavor CRISCO® all-vegetable shortening plus additional for greasing**
1 **package (3 ounces) cream cheese, softened**
1 **tablespoon milk**
¼ **cup firmly packed brown sugar**
½ **cup apricot preserves**
1¼ **cups all-purpose flour**
1½ **teaspoons baking powder**
1½ **teaspoons ground cinnamon**
¼ **teaspoon salt**
½ **cup coarsely chopped pecans or flake coconut**

FROSTING

1 **cup confectioners' sugar**
¼ **cup apricot preserves**
1 **tablespoon Butter Flavor* CRISCO® Stick or 1 tablespoon Butter Flavor CRISCO® all-vegetable shortening**
Flake coconut or finely chopped pecans (optional)

*Butter Flavor Crisco is artificially flavored.

1. Heat oven to 350°F. Grease baking sheets with shortening. Place sheets of foil on countertop for cooling cookies. Cream ½ cup shortening, cream cheese and milk at medium speed of electric mixer until well blended. Beat in brown sugar. Beat in preserves.

2. Combine flour, baking powder, cinnamon and salt. Mix into creamed mixture. Stir in nuts. Drop 2 level measuring tablespoons of dough into a mound to form each cookie. Place 2 inches apart on baking sheets.

3. Bake one baking sheet at a time at 350°F for 14 minutes. *Do not overbake.* Cool on baking sheet one minute. Remove cookies to foil to cool completely.

4. For frosting, combine confectioners' sugar, preserves and shortening in small mixing bowl. Beat with electric mixer until well blended. Frost cooled cookies. Sprinkle coconut over frosting, if desired.

Makes 1½ dozen cookies

Tip: Try peach or pineapple preserves in place of apricot.

Prep Time: 25 minutes
Bake Time: 14 minutes

Never store two different kinds of cookies in the same container because their flavors and textures can change.

QUICK PEANUT BUTTER CHOCOLATE CHIP COOKIES

**1 package DUNCAN HINES® Moist
Deluxe Yellow Cake Mix**
½ cup creamy peanut butter
½ cup butter or margarine, softened
2 eggs
1 cup milk chocolate chips

1. Preheat oven to 350°F. Grease cookie sheets.

2. Combine cake mix, peanut butter, butter and eggs in large bowl. Mix at low speed with electric mixer until blended. Stir in chocolate chips.

3. Drop by rounded teaspoonfuls onto prepared cookie sheets. Bake 9 to 11 minutes or until lightly browned. Cool 2 minutes on cookie sheets. Remove to cooling racks.

Makes about 4 dozen cookies

Tip: Crunchy peanut butter may be substituted for regular peanut butter.

Angel Pillow

SPICY GINGERBREAD COOKIES

COOKIES
¾ cup (1½ sticks) butter, softened
⅔ cup light molasses
½ cup firmly packed brown sugar
1 egg
1½ teaspoons grated lemon peel
2½ cups all-purpose flour
1¼ teaspoons ground cinnamon
1 teaspoon ground allspice
1 teaspoon vanilla
½ teaspoon baking soda
½ teaspoon salt
½ teaspoon ground ginger
¼ teaspoon baking powder

FROSTING
4 cups powdered sugar
½ cup (1 stick) butter, softened
4 tablespoons milk
2 teaspoons vanilla

For cookies, combine butter, molasses, brown sugar, egg and lemon peel in large bowl. Beat at medium speed until smooth and creamy. Add all remaining cookie ingredients. Reduce speed to low; beat well. Cover; refrigerate at least 2 hours.

Preheat oven to 350°F. Roll out dough, one half at a time, on well floured surface to ¼-inch thickness. (Keep remaining dough refrigerated.) Cut out dough with 3- to 4-inch cookie cutters. Place on greased cookie sheets. Bake 6 to 8 minutes or until no indentation remains when touched. Remove immediately. Cool.

For frosting, combine powdered sugar, butter, milk and vanilla in small bowl. Beat at low speed until fluffy. Frost cookies.
Makes about 4 dozen cookies

PEANUT BUTTER JUMBOS

½ cup butter, softened
1 cup packed brown sugar
1 cup granulated sugar
1½ cups peanut butter
3 eggs
2 teaspoons baking soda
1 teaspoon vanilla
4½ cups uncooked rolled oats
1 cup (6 ounces) semisweet chocolate chips
1 cup candy-coated chocolate pieces

Preheat oven to 350°F. Lightly grease cookie sheets or line with parchment paper.

Beat butter, sugars, peanut butter and eggs in large bowl until well blended. Blend in baking soda, vanilla and oats until well mixed. Stir in chocolate chips and candy pieces.

Scoop out about ⅓ cup dough for each cookie. Place on prepared cookie sheets, spacing about 4 inches apart. Press each cookie to flatten slightly. Bake 15 to 20 minutes or until firm in center. Remove to wire racks to cool.
Makes about 1½ dozen cookies

Peanut Butter Jumbo Sandwiches: Prepare cookies as directed. Place ⅓ cup softened chocolate or vanilla ice cream on cookie bottom. Top with cookie. Lightly press sandwich together. Repeat with remaining cookies. Wrap sandwiches in plastic wrap; freeze until firm.

JAM–UP OATMEAL COOKIES

1 Butter Flavor* CRISCO® Stick or 1 cup
    Butter Flavor CRISCO® all-vegetable
    shortening plus additional for
    greasing
1½ cups firmly packed brown sugar
2 eggs
2 teaspoons almond extract
2 cups all-purpose flour
1 teaspoon baking powder
1 teaspoon salt
½ teaspoon baking soda
2½ cups quick oats (not instant or
    old-fashioned), uncooked
1 cup finely chopped pecans
1 jar (12 ounces) strawberry jam
    Sugar for sprinkling

Butter Flavor Crisco is artificially flavored.

1. Combine 1 cup shortening and brown sugar in large bowl. Beat at medium speed of electric mixer until well blended. Beat in eggs and almond extract.

2. Combine flour, baking powder, salt and baking soda. Mix into shortening mixture at low speed until just blended. Stir in oats and chopped nuts with spoon. Cover and refrigerate at least 1 hour.

3. Heat oven to 350°F. Grease baking sheets with shortening. Place sheets of foil on countertop for cooling cookies.

4. Roll out dough, half at a time, to about ¼-inch thickness on floured surface. Cut out with 2½-inch round cookie cutter. Place 1 teaspoonful of jam in center of half of the rounds. Top with remaining rounds. Press edges to seal. Prick centers; sprinkle with sugar. Place 1 inch apart on baking sheets.

5. Bake one baking sheet at a time at 350°F for 12 to 15 minutes or until lightly browned. *Do not overbake.* Cool 2 minutes on baking sheets. Remove cookies to foil to cool completely.
Makes about 2 dozen cookies

DOUBLE CHOCOLATE OAT COOKIES

1 package (12 ounces) semi-sweet
    chocolate pieces, divided (about
    2 cups)
½ cup margarine or butter, softened
½ cup sugar
1 egg
¼ teaspoon vanilla
¾ cup all-purpose flour
¾ cup QUAKER® Oats (quick or old
    fashioned, uncooked)
1 teaspoon baking powder
¼ teaspoon baking soda
¼ teaspoon salt (optional)

Preheat oven to 375°F. Melt 1 cup chocolate pieces in small saucepan; set aside. Beat margarine and sugar until fluffy; add melted chocolate, egg and vanilla. Add combined flour, oats, baking powder, baking soda and salt; mix well. Stir in remaining chocolate pieces. Drop by rounded tablespoonfuls onto ungreased cookie sheet. Bake 8 to 10 minutes. Cool 1 minute on cookie sheet; remove to wire rack.
Makes about 3 dozen cookies

BUTTER DROP–INS

COOKIES
- ½ **Butter Flavor* CRISCO® Stick or ½ cup Butter Flavor CRISCO® all-vegetable shortening plus additional for greasing**
- ¾ **cup granulated sugar**
- 1 **tablespoon milk**
- 1 **egg**
- ½ **teaspoon vanilla extract**
- 1¼ **cups all-purpose flour**
- ¼ **teaspoon salt**
- ¼ **teaspoon baking powder**

FROSTING
- ½ **Butter Flavor* CRISCO® Stick or ½ cup Butter Flavor CRISCO® all-vegetable shortening**
- 1 **pound (4 cups) confectioners' sugar**
- ⅓ **cup milk**
- 1 **teaspoon vanilla extract**

*Butter Flavor Crisco is artificially flavored.

1. Heat oven to 375°F. Grease baking sheets. Place sheets of foil on countertop for cooling cookies.

2. Combine ½ cup shortening, granulated sugar and milk in medium bowl at medium speed of electric mixer until well blended. Beat in egg and vanilla. Combine flour, salt and baking powder. Mix into creamed mixture.

3. Drop level measuring tablespoonfuls 2 inches apart onto baking sheet. Bake one baking sheet at a time at 375°F for 7 to 9 minutes. Remove cookies to foil to cool completely.

4. For frosting, combine shortening, confectioners' sugar, milk and vanilla in small mixing bowl. Beat at low speed of electric mixer for 15 seconds. Scrape bowl. Beat at high speed for 2 minutes, or until smooth and creamy. Frost cookies.

Makes 1½ to 2 dozen cookies

Note: Frosting can be tinted with food coloring and piped decoratively onto cookies, if desired.

Prep Time: 20 minutes
Bake Time: 7 to 9 minutes

MINI PIZZA COOKIES

- 1 **(20-ounce) tube of refrigerated sugar cookie dough**
- 2 **cups (16 ounces) prepared pink frosting "M&M's"® Chocolate Mini Baking Bits Variety of additional toppings such as shredded coconut, granola, raisins, nuts, small pretzels, snack mixes, sunflower seeds, popped corn and mini marshmallows**

Preheat oven to 350°F. Lightly grease cookie sheets; set aside. Divide dough into 8 equal portions. On lightly floured surface, roll each portion of dough into ¼-inch-thick circle; place about 2 inches apart onto prepared cookie sheets. Bake 10 to 13 minutes or until golden brown on edges. Cool completely on wire racks. Spread top of each pizza with frosting; sprinkle with "M&M's"® Chocolate Mini Baking Bits and 2 or 3 suggested toppings.

Makes 8 cookies

Mini Pizza Cookie

BURIED CHERRY COOKIES

Chocolate Frosting (recipe follows)
½ cup butter or margarine, softened
1 cup sugar
1 egg
1½ teaspoons vanilla extract
1½ cups all-purpose flour
⅓ cup HERSHEY'S Cocoa
¼ teaspoon baking powder
¼ teaspoon baking soda
¼ teaspoon salt
1 jar (10 ounces) small maraschino
    cherries, drained

1. Prepare Chocolate Frosting; set aside. Heat oven to 350°F.

2. Beat butter, sugar, egg and vanilla in large bowl until light and fluffy. Stir together flour, cocoa, baking powder, baking soda and salt; gradually add to butter mixture, beating until well blended.

3. Shape dough into 1-inch balls. Place on ungreased cookie sheet about 2 inches apart. Press thumb in center of each ball to make indentation; place one cherry in each thumbprint.

4. Bake 10 minutes or until edges are set. Remove from cookie sheet to wire rack. Cool completely. Spoon scant teaspoonful frosting over each cherry, spreading to cover cherry.
Makes about 3½ dozen cookies

Chocolate Frosting: Place ⅔ cups sweetened condensed milk (not evaporated milk) and ½ cup HERSHEY'S Semi-Sweet Chocolate Chips in small microwave-safe bowl; stir. Microwave at HIGH (100%) 1 minute or until chips are melted and mixture is smooth when stirred. Cool completely. Makes 1 cup frosting.

GIANT PEANUT BUTTER CUP COOKIES

½ cup (1 stick) butter or margarine,
    softened
¾ cup sugar
⅓ cup REESE'S Creamy or Crunchy
    Peanut Butter
1 egg
½ teaspoon vanilla extract
1¼ cups all-purpose flour
½ teaspoon baking soda
¼ teaspoon salt
16 REESE'S Peanut Butter Cup
    Miniatures, cut into fourths

1. Heat oven to 350°F.

2. Beat beat butter, sugar and peanut butter in small mixer bowl until creamy. Add egg and vanilla; beat well. Stir together flour, baking soda and salt. Add to butter mixture; blend well. Drop dough by level ¼ cup measurements onto ungreased cookie sheets, three cookies per sheet. (Cookies will spread while baking.) Push about seven pieces of peanut butter cup into each cookie, flattening cookie slightly.

3. Bake 15 to 17 minutes or until light golden brown around the edges. Centers will be pale and slightly soft. Cool 1 minute on cookie sheet. Remove to wire rack; cool completely.
Makes 9 cookies

Giant Peanut Butter Cup Cookie

BROWNIE TURTLE COOKIES

2 squares (1 ounce each) unsweetened
    baking chocolate
⅓ cup solid vegetable shortening
1 cup granulated sugar
½ teaspoon vanilla extract
2 large eggs
1¼ cups all-purpose flour
½ teaspoon baking powder
½ teaspoon salt
1 cup "M&M's"® Milk Chocolate Mini
    Baking Bits, divided
1 cup pecan halves
⅓ cup caramel ice cream topping
⅓ cup shredded coconut
⅓ cup finely chopped pecans

Preheat oven to 350°F. Lightly grease cookie
sheets; set aside. Heat chocolate and shortening
in 2-quart saucepan over low heat, stirring
constantly until melted; remove from heat.
Mix in sugar, vanilla and eggs. Blend in
flour, baking powder and salt. Stir in ⅔ cup
"M&M's"® Milk Chocolate Mini Baking Bits.
For each cookie, arrange 3 pecan halves, with
ends almost touching at center, on prepared
cookie sheets. Drop dough by rounded
teaspoonfuls onto center of each group of
pecans; mound the dough slightly. Bake
8 to 10 minutes just until set. *Do not overbake.*
Cool completely on wire racks. In small bowl
combine ice cream topping, coconut and nuts;
top each cookie with about 1½ teaspoons
mixture. Press remaining ⅓ cup "M&M's"®
Milk Chocolate Mini Baking Bits into topping.
    Makes about 2½ dozen cookies

HAYSTACKS

¼ Butter Flavor* CRISCO® Stick or ¼ cup
    Butter Flavor CRISCO® all-vegetable
    shortening
½ cup creamy peanut butter
2 cups butterscotch-flavored chips
6 cups corn flakes
⅔ cup semisweet miniature chocolate
    chips
    Chopped peanuts or chocolate jimmies
    (optional)

*Butter Flavor Crisco is artificially flavored.

1. Combine ¼ cup shortening, peanut butter
and butterscotch chips in large microwave-safe
bowl. Cover with waxed paper. Microwave at
50% (MEDIUM). Stir after 1 minute. Repeat
until smooth (or melt on rangetop in small
saucepan on very low heat, stirring
constantly).

2. Pour corn flakes into large bowl. Pour hot
butterscotch mixture over flakes. Stir with
spoon until flakes are coated. Stir in chocolate
chips.

3. Spoon ¼ cup of the mixture into mounds
on waxed paper-lined baking sheets. Sprinkle
with chopped nuts, if desired. Refrigerate
until firm.   *Makes about 3 dozen cookies*

Brownie Turtle Cookie

BLISSFUL BARS

PHILADELPHIA® MARBLE BROWNIES

1 package (21½ ounces) brownie mix
1 package (8 ounces) PHILADELPHIA® Cream Cheese, softened
⅓ cup sugar
½ teaspoon vanilla
1 egg
1 cup BAKER'S® Semi-Sweet Real Chocolate Chips

PREPARE brownie mix as directed on package. Spread into greased 13×9-inch baking pan.

MIX cream cheese, sugar and vanilla with electric mixer on medium speed until well blended. Add egg; mix well. Pour over brownie mixture; cut through batter with knife several times for marble effect. Sprinkle with chips.

BAKE at 350°F for 35 to 40 minutes or until cream cheese mixture is lightly browned. Cool in pan on wire rack. Cut into squares.

Makes 24 brownies

Prep Time: 20 minutes plus cooling
Bake Time: 40 minutes

Philadelphia® Marble Brownies

Tropical Coconut Squares

1 cup butter, softened
½ cup granulated sugar
2 egg yolks
¼ teaspoon salt
2¼ cups plus 3 tablespoons all-purpose flour, divided
½ teaspoon baking powder
1½ cups packed light brown sugar
3 eggs
1 teaspoon vanilla
1½ cups macadamia nuts
2 cups flaked coconut

Preheat oven to 350°F. Grease 15×10-inch jelly-roll pan.

Beat butter and granulated sugar in large bowl with electric mixer at medium speed until light and fluffy. Beat in egg yolks and salt. Gradually add 2¼ cups flour; beat at low speed until well blended. Spread dough in prepared pan. Bake 16 to 18 minutes or until golden brown.

Meanwhile, combine remaining 3 tablespoons flour and baking powder in small bowl. Beat brown sugar and eggs in large bowl with electric mixer at medium speed until very thick. Beat in vanilla. Gradually add flour mixture; beat at low speed until well blended. Stir in nuts.

Spread batter evenly over hot crust; sprinkle with coconut. Return pan to oven; bake 20 to 22 minutes or until topping is golden brown and puffed. Remove pan to wire rack to cool completely. Cut into 2-inch squares. Store squares tightly covered at room temperature or freeze up to 3 months.

Makes about 40 squares

"Cordially Yours" Chocolate Chip Bars

¾ Butter Flavor* CRISCO® Stick or ¾ cup Butter Flavor Crisco® all-vegetable shortening plus additional for greasing
2 eggs
½ cup granulated sugar
¼ cup firmly packed brown sugar
1½ teaspoons vanilla extract
1 teaspoon almond extract
2 cups all-purpose flour
1 teaspoon baking soda
½ teaspoon cinnamon
1 can (21 ounces) cherry pie filling
1½ cups milk chocolate chips
Powdered sugar

Butter Flavor Crisco is artificially flavored.

1. Preheat oven to 350°F. Grease 15½×10½×1-inch pan.

2. Combine ¾ cup shortening, eggs, granulated sugar, brown sugar, vanilla and almond extract in large bowl. Beat at medium speed of electric mixer until well blended.

3. Combine flour, baking soda and cinnamon. Mix into creamed mixture at low speed until just blended. Stir in pie filling and chocolate chips. Spread in pan.

4. Bake 25 minutes or until lightly browned and top springs back when lightly pressed. Cool completely in pan on wire rack. Sprinkle with powdered sugar. Cut into 2½×2-inch bars.
Makes 30 bars

Tropical Coconut Squares

RICH AND FUDGY FROSTED BROWNIES

8 ounces unsweetened chocolate
1 cup butter
3 cups sugar
5 eggs
2 tablespoons light corn syrup
1 tablespoon vanilla extract
1¾ cups all-purpose flour
1 cup coarsely chopped nuts (optional)
Frosting (recipe follows)

Preheat oven to 375°F. Melt chocolate and butter in medium saucepan over low heat, stirring constantly. Set aside and let cool. Beat sugar, eggs, corn syrup and vanilla in large bowl with electric mixer on high speed 10 minutes. Blend in chocolate mixture on low speed. Add flour, beating just until blended. Stir in nuts, if desired. Spread in greased 13×9-inch pan. Bake 30 to 35 minutes. *Do not overbake.* Cool completely before frosting.

Makes 24 brownies

FROSTING

6 tablespoons butter or margarine, softened
⅓ cup unsweetened cocoa powder
2⅔ cups powdered sugar
⅓ cup milk
1 tablespoon vanilla extract

Beat butter in small bowl until creamy. Add cocoa and powdered sugar alternately with milk; beat until frosting is of spreading consistency. Stir in vanilla. Spread on cooled brownies.

Favorite recipe from **Bob Evans**®

CHEWY RED RASPBERRY BARS

1 cup firmly packed light brown sugar
½ cup butter or margarine, room temperature
½ teaspoon almond extract
1 cup all-purpose flour
1 cup quick-cooking or old-fashioned oats
1 teaspoon baking powder
½ cup SMUCKER'S® Red Raspberry Preserves

Combine brown sugar and butter; beat until fluffy. Beat in almond extract. Mix in flour, oats and baking powder until crumbly. Reserve ¼ cup mixture; pat remaining mixture into bottom of greased 8-inch square baking pan. Dot preserves over crumb mixture in pan; sprinkle with reserved crumb mixture.

Bake at 350°F for 30 to 40 minutes or until brown. Cool on wire rack. Cut into bars.

Makes 12 bars

Replacing the butter or margarine in a recipe with a spread, diet margarine, whipped butter or whipped margarine may result in an inferior cookie or brownie. For best results, use the product called for in the recipe.

DOUBLE CHOCOLATE CRISPY BARS

6 cups crispy rice cereal
½ cup peanut butter
⅓ cup butter
2 squares (1 ounce each) unsweetened
   chocolate
1 package (8 ounces) marshmallows
1 cup (6 ounces) semisweet chocolate
   chips *or* 6 ounces bittersweet
   chocolate, chopped
6 ounces white chocolate, chopped
2 teaspoons shortening, divided

Preheat oven to 350°F. Line 13×9-inch pan with waxed paper; set aside. Spread cereal on cookie sheet; toast in oven 10 minutes or until crispy; place in large bowl. Meanwhile, mix peanut butter, butter and unsweetened chocolate in large heavy saucepan. Stir over low heat until chocolate is melted. Add marshmallows; stir until melted and smooth. Pour chocolate mixture over cereal; mix until evenly coated. Press firmly into prepared pan. Place semisweet and white chocolates into separate bowls. Add 1 teaspoon shortening to each bowl. Place bowls over very warm water; stir until chocolates are melted. Spread top of bars with melted semisweet chocolate; cool until chocolate is set. Turn bars out of pan onto waxed paper, chocolate side down. Remove waxed paper from bottom of bars; spread white chocolate over surface. Cool until chocolate is set. Cut into 2×1½-inch bars.

Makes about 3 dozen bars

MARBLED PEANUT BUTTER BROWNIES

⅔ cup all-purpose or whole wheat flour
½ teaspoon baking powder
¼ teaspoon salt
¾ cup firmly packed brown sugar
½ cup SMUCKER'S® Creamy Natural
   Peanut Butter or LAURA
   SCUDDER'S® Smooth Old-Fashioned
   Peanut Butter
¼ cup butter or margarine, softened
2 eggs
1 teaspoon vanilla
3 (1-ounce) squares semisweet chocolate
   or ½ cup semisweet chocolate chips,
   melted and cooled

Combine flour, baking powder and salt; set aside.

In small bowl of electric mixer, combine brown sugar, peanut butter and butter; beat until light and creamy. Add eggs and vanilla; beat until fluffy. Stir in flour mixture just until blended. Spread in greased 8-inch square baking pan. Drizzle chocolate over batter, then swirl into batter with table knife to marbleize.

Bake in preheated 350°F oven 25 to 30 minutes or until toothpick inserted in center comes out clean. Cool in pan on wire rack. Cut into bars.

Makes 24 bars

GOOEY CARAMEL CHOCOLATE BARS

2 cups all-purpose flour
1 cup granulated sugar
¼ teaspoon salt
2 cups (4 sticks) butter, divided
1 cup packed light brown sugar
⅓ cup light corn syrup
1 cup (6 ounces) semisweet chocolate chips

Preheat oven to 350°F. Line 13×9-inch baking pan with foil. Combine flour, granulated sugar and salt in medium bowl; stir until blended. Cut in 14 tablespoons (1¾ sticks) butter until mixture resembles coarse crumbs. Press onto bottom of prepared pan.

Bake 18 to 20 minutes or until lightly browned around edges. Remove pan to wire rack; cool completely.

Combine 1 cup (2 sticks) butter, brown sugar and corn syrup in heavy medium saucepan. Cook over medium heat 5 to 8 minutes or until mixture boils, stirring frequently. Boil gently 2 minutes, without stirring. Immediately pour over cooled base; spread evenly to edges of pan with metal spatula. Cool completely.

Melt chocolate in double boiler over hot (not boiling) water. Stir in remaining 2 tablespoons butter. Pour over cooled caramel layer and spread evenly to edges of pan with metal spatula. Refrigerate 10 to 15 minutes until chocolate begins to set. Remove; cool completely. Cut into bars.

Makes 3 dozen bars

RASPBERRY WALNUT BARS

1¾ cups all-purpose flour, divided
¾ cup margarine or butter, softened
1⅓ cups packed light brown sugar, divided
½ cup raspberry preserves
½ cup egg substitute
1 teaspoon salt
1 teaspoon DAVIS® Baking Powder
½ cup PLANTERS® Walnuts, chopped
Powdered Sugar Glaze (recipe follows, optional)

1. Mix 1½ cups flour, margarine and ⅓ cup brown sugar in large bowl with mixer at low speed; press mixture onto bottom of ungreased 13×9×2-inch baking pan.

2. Bake in preheated 350°F oven for 18 to 20 minutes. Spread raspberry preserves over baked layer.

3. Mix remaining flour, brown sugar, egg substitute, salt and baking powder in medium bowl. Spread over raspberry layer; sprinkle with walnuts.

4. Bake at 350°F for 18 to 20 minutes or until done. Cool on wire rack. Drizzle with Powdered Sugar Glaze, if desired. Cut into bars. *Makes 2 dozen bars*

Powdered Sugar Glaze: Combine 1 cup powdered sugar and 5 to 6 teaspoons water.

Preparation Time: 20 minutes
Cook Time: 36 minutes
Total Time: 56 minutes

MISSISSIPPI MUD BARS

¾ cup packed brown sugar
½ cup butter, softened
1 egg
1 teaspoon vanilla
½ teaspoon baking soda
¼ teaspoon salt
1 cup plus 2 tablespoons all-purpose flour
1 cup (6 ounces) semisweet chocolate chips, divided
1 cup (6 ounces) white chocolate chips, divided
½ cup chopped walnuts or pecans

Preheat oven to 375°F. Line a 9-inch square pan with foil; grease foil. Beat sugar and butter in large bowl until blended and smooth. Beat in egg and vanilla until light. Blend in baking soda and salt. Add flour, mixing until well blended. Stir in ¾ cup each semisweet and white chocolate chips and nuts. Spread dough in prepared pan. Bake 23 to 25 minutes or until center feels firm. *Do not overbake.* Remove from oven; sprinkle remaining ¼ cup each semisweet and white chocolate chips over top. Let stand until chips melt; spread evenly over bars. Cool in pan on wire rack until chocolate is set. Cut into 2×1-inch bars.

Makes about 3 dozen bars

ooey Caramel Chocolate Bars

Buttery Lemon Bars

CRUST
1¼ cups all-purpose flour
½ cup butter, softened
¼ cup powdered sugar
½ teaspoon vanilla

FILLING
1 cup granulated sugar
2 eggs
⅓ cup fresh lemon juice
2 tablespoons all-purpose flour
Grated peel of 1 lemon
Powdered sugar

1. Preheat oven to 350°F.

2. Combine all crust ingredients in small bowl. Beat at low speed 2 to 3 minutes until mixture is crumbly. Press onto bottom of 8-inch square baking pan. Bake 15 to 20 minutes or until edges are lightly browned.

3. Combine all filling ingredients except powdered sugar in small bowl. Beat at low speed until well mixed.

4. Pour filling over hot crust. Continue baking 15 to 18 minutes or until filling is set. Sprinkle with powdered sugar; cool completely. Cut into bars; sprinkle again with powdered sugar. *Makes about 16 bars*

Hershey's Premium Double Chocolate Brownies

¾ cup HERSHEY'S Cocoa
½ teaspoon baking soda
⅔ cup butter or margarine, melted and divided
½ cup boiling water
2 cups sugar
2 eggs
1 teaspoon vanilla extract
1⅓ cups all-purpose flour
¼ teaspoon salt
2 cups (12-ounce package) HERSHEY'S Semi-Sweet Chocolate Chips
½ cup coarsely chopped nuts (optional)

1. Heat oven to 350°F. Grease 13×9×2-inch baking pan.

2. Stir together cocoa and baking soda in large bowl; stir in ⅓ cup butter. Add boiling water; stir until mixture thickens. Stir in sugar, eggs, remaining ⅓ cup butter and vanilla; stir until smooth. Gradually add flour and salt to cocoa mixture, beating until well blended. Stir in chocolate chips and nuts, if desired; pour batter into prepared pan.

3. Bake 35 to 40 minutes or until brownies begin to pull away from sides of pan. Cool completely in pan on wire rack. Cut into bars. *Makes about 36 brownies*

CRISPY CHOCOLATE BARS

1 package (6 ounces, 1 cup) semi-sweet
   chocolate chips
1 package (6 ounces, 1 cup) butterscotch
   chips
½ cup peanut butter
5 cups KELLOGG'S® CORN FLAKES®
   cereal
   Vegetable cooking spray

1. In large saucepan, combine chocolate and
butterscotch chips and peanut butter. Stir over
low heat until smooth. Remove from heat.

2. Add Kellogg's Corn Flakes® cereal. Stir until
well coated.

3. Using buttered spatula or waxed paper,
press mixture evenly into 9×9×2-inch pan
coated with cooking spray. Cut into bars when
cool. *Makes 16 bars*

*For easy removal of brownies and bar cookies
(and no cleanup!), line the baking pan with
foil and leave at least 2 inches of foil hanging
over on each end. After baking, use the foil to
lift the brownies or bars out of the pan. Place
brownies or bars on a cutting board, remove
the foil and cut the treats into pieces.*

DOUBLE CHOCOLATE BARS

1½ cups all-purpose flour
¼ cup unsweetened cocoa
1 teaspoon baking soda
½ cup FLEISCHMANN'S® Original
   Margarine, softened
¾ cup packed dark brown sugar
½ cup granulated sugar
¼ cup EGG BEATERS® Healthy Real Egg
   Product
1 teaspoon vanilla extract
1 cup reduced-fat chocolate-flavored
   baking chips

1. Mix flour, cocoa and baking soda in small
bowl; set aside.

2. Blend margarine, sugars, Egg Beaters® and
vanilla in large bowl with mixer at medium
speed until smooth. Stir in flour mixture until
blended; stir in chips. Press dough in greased
13×9×2-inch baking pan.

3. Bake in preheated 350°F oven for 18
minutes or until done. Cool completely on
wire rack; cut into bars. *Makes 32 bars*

Preparation Time: 15 minutes
Cook Time: 18 minutes
Total Time: 33 minutes

Pecan Pie Bars

¾ cup butter, softened
½ cup powdered sugar
1½ cups all-purpose flour
3 eggs
2 cups coarsely chopped pecans
1 cup granulated sugar
1 cup light corn syrup
2 tablespoons butter, melted
1 teaspoon vanilla

Preheat oven to 350°F. For crust, beat butter in large bowl with electric mixer at medium speed until smooth. Add powdered sugar; beat at medium speed until well blended.

Add flour gradually, beating at low speed after each addition. (Mixture will be crumbly but presses together easily.)

Press dough evenly into ungreased 13×9-inch baking pan. Press mixture slightly up sides of pan (less than ¼ inch) to form lip to hold filling. Bake 20 to 25 minutes or until golden brown.

Meanwhile, for filling, beat eggs in medium bowl with fork. Add pecans, granulated sugar, corn syrup, melted butter and vanilla; mix well.

Pour filling over partially baked crust. Return to oven; bake 35 to 40 minutes or until filling is set.

Loosen edges with knife. Let cool completely on wire rack before cutting into squares. Cover and refrigerate until 10 to 15 minutes before serving time. (Do not freeze.)

Makes about 48 bars

Spiced Date Bars

½ cup margarine, softened
1 cup packed brown sugar
2 eggs
¾ cup light sour cream
2 cups all-purpose flour
1 teaspoon baking soda
1 teaspoon ground cinnamon
½ teaspoon ground nutmeg
1 package (8 or 10 ounces) DOLE®
   Chopped Dates or Pitted Dates,
   chopped
Powdered sugar (optional)

• Beat margarine and brown sugar until light and fluffy. Beat in eggs, one at a time. Stir in sour cream.

• Combine dry ingredients. Beat into sour cream, stir in dates. Spread batter evenly into greased 13×9-inch baking pan.

• Bake at 350°F 25 to 30 minutes or until toothpick inserted in center comes out clean. Cool completely in pan on wire rack. Cut into bars. Dust with powdered sugar.

Makes 24 bars

Prep Time: 15 minutes
Bake Time: 30 minutes

Pecan Pie Bars

CHOCOLATE CHIP BROWNIES

¾ cup granulated sugar
½ cup butter
2 tablespoons water
2 cups semisweet chocolate chips or mini chocolate chips, divided
1½ teaspoons vanilla
1¼ cups all-purpose flour
½ teaspoon baking soda
½ teaspoon salt
2 eggs
Powdered sugar (optional)

Preheat oven to 350°F. Grease 9-inch square baking pan.

Combine sugar, butter and water in medium microwavable mixing bowl. Microwave on HIGH 2½ to 3 minutes or until butter is melted. Stir in 1 cup chocolate chips; stir gently until chips are melted and mixture is well blended. Stir in vanilla; let stand 5 minutes to cool.

Combine flour, baking soda and salt in small bowl. Beat eggs into chocolate mixture, 1 at a time. Add flour mixture; mix well. Stir in remaining 1 cup chocolate chips. Spread batter evenly into prepared pan.

Bake 25 minutes for fudgy brownies or 30 to 35 minutes for cakelike brownies. Remove pan to wire rack to cool completely. Cut into 2¼-inch squares. Place powdered sugar in fine-mesh strainer and sprinkle over brownies, if desired. Store tightly covered at room temperature or freeze up to 3 months.

Makes 16 browni

Chocolate Chip Brownies

EAGLE BRAND

Cookies & Treats

The Magic of Eagle® Brand

For over 145 years, Eagle Brand has been America's #1 trusted brand of sweetened condensed milk. Since 1856, bakers have been depending on all-natural Eagle® Brand Sweetened Condensed Milk to help them make all kinds of indulgent desserts and sweet treats. There are three varieties of Eagle Brand: Original, introduced in 1856; Low Fat, introduced in 1994; and Fat Free, introduced in 1995. All three provide the rich, creamy, sweet taste that's the delicious secret to making fabulous desserts, candies, beverages and treats. Eagle Brand has been developing and creating deliciously foolproof recipes for decades.

THE MAGIC INGREDIENT

Beginners and experienced cooks alike love making treats with Eagle Brand because it guarantees success. It is a special blend of milk and sugar that is condensed by a unique vacuum process to create a "foolproof" base for a variety of recipes. Many recipes that use Eagle Brand require

82

no additional sugar because it contains sugar that has been thoroughly dissolved during manufacturing, resulting in timesaving steps. Eagle Brand has a magical thickening quality too. When it is combined with acidic fruit juice, such as lemon, lime or orange juice, it thickens—without heating—to form rich and creamy pie fillings, puddings and cheesecakes. When heated with chocolate, Eagle Brand quickly thickens to a velvety smooth consistency for candies and sauces that are never grainy or long-cooking. Remember: Evaporated milk is completely different than Eagle Brand and cannot be substituted for it.

MAKE MAGIC IN MINUTES

There's no easier way to bring magic into your day than with Eagle Brand. Turn the pages of this publication and you'll find a variety of recipes perfect to make any time of year. There are holiday favorites like Festive Cranberry Bars and Peanut Blossom Cookies, as well as any-day treats like Magic Cookie Bars and Double Chocolate Brownies. Marbled Cheesecake Bars are a great way to end a spring luncheon, and Lemon Crumb Bars are

Magic Cookie Bars, page 92

refreshing on a hot summer afternoon. There are even fabulous no-bake recipes for those days when just the thought of turning on the oven is too much to bear. So whether you're craving a classic Eagle Brand treat, like Foolproof Dark Chocolate Fudge, or you want to try something new, like Butterscotch Apple Squares, with these recipes and Eagle Brand, you'll be making magic in minutes!

EAGLE® BRAND ON THE INTERNET

For more information and recipes using Eagle® Brand Sweetened Condensed Milk, visit our website at www.eaglebrand.com.

HINTS FOR USING EAGLE BRAND

KEEPING IT FRESH
Store unopened cans of Eagle Brand in a cool dry place—
not near the range. Because it is a natural product, Eagle
Brand may vary in color and consistency from can to can. It
will become thicker and more caramel-colored when kept
on the shelf for a long time. These changes will not affect its
quality, simply stir briskly before using. If you don't need
the whole can for a recipe, measure the desired amount
and place the remainder in a glass or plastic storage
container. Cover it tightly and keep it in the refrigerator. It
will stay fresh about one week.

MELTING CHOCOLATE
Chocolate melts smoothly and easily with Eagle Brand. For
the smoothest texture, be sure to use a medium to heavy
saucepan and low heat. As the chocolate heats, stir the
mixture constantly until it is smooth. If the heat is too high,
the chocolate may form tiny clumps.

MAKING CARAMEL

For an easy caramel topping or dip,
simply heat Eagle Brand and serve it
over ice cream or with assorted
cookies and fruit. Just follow one of
these easy methods:

© The Borden Company 1940

Oven: Preheat the oven to 425°F.
Pour 1 can Eagle Brand into a 9-inch
pie plate. Cover with foil; place in a
larger shallow pan. Fill the larger
pan with hot water. Bake 1 hour or
until Eagle Brand is thick and
caramel-colored. Beat until smooth.

Stovetop: Pour 1 can Eagle Brand into the top of a double
boiler; place over boiling water. Over low heat, simmer 1 to
1½ hours or until thick and caramel-colored, stirring
occasionally. Beat until smooth.

Microwave: Pour 1 can Eagle Brand into a 2-quart microwave-safe glass measuring cup. Cook on 50% power (MEDIUM) 4 minutes, stirring briskly every 2 minutes until smooth. Cook on 30% power (MEDIUM-LOW) 20 to 26 minutes or until very thick and caramel-colored. Stir briskly every 4 minutes during the first 16 minutes, and every 2 minutes during the last 4 to 10 minutes. *Caution: Never heat an unopened can.*

GIFT GIVING MADE EASY

Easy Chocolate Truffles, page 145

Homemade treats become gorgeous gifts when arranged in unique packages wrapped in festive papers and decorated with ribbons or bows. Show someone how much you care by wrapping delicious Eagle Brand treats in fun, festive containers from around the house.

Plates & Bowls: Choose a festive plate, tray or bowl—from paper, to crockery, to the fanciest china—then stack the sweets high and wrap it all up with clear or colored plastic wrap or cellophane. Attach some pretty ribbons or a big bow and the gift is ready for giving.

Boxes & Tins: Boxes and tins come in a variety of shapes and sizes and are the perfect containers for cookies, bars and candies. Line the box or tin with tissue paper and then fill with tasty goodies. For a special touch, tuck candies or small cookies into colored paper or foil liners before placing them in the container.

Baskets: Baskets are versatile and are available in a large array of shapes, sizes and materials. Simply line the basket with pretty paper or cloth napkins and pile in the treats.

Glass Jars: Large, wide-mouthed canning jars are great for dessert sauces. Fill them to the brim and slip rounds of colorful cloth between the lids and the metal screw bands.

Irresistible Classics

*W*ho can resist Magic Cookie Bars, Chocolate Chip Treasure Cookies or Foolproof Dark Chocolate Fudge? No one can! These are just a few of the Eagle® Brand classics that have been loved by families for generations. Try one of these fabulous bars or sensational cookies and you'll discover how Eagle® Brand "Makes Magic in Minutes." We've even included some fun variations so you can create a new twist on your favorite classic. Versatile Cut-Out Cookies, Lemon Crumb Bars—the list of favorites goes on and on!

Double Delicious Cookie Bars *(page 88)*

Double Delicious Cookie Bars

Prep Time: 10 minutes   **Bake Time:** 25 to 30 minutes

½ cup (1 stick) butter or margarine
1½ cups graham cracker crumbs
1 (14-ounce) can EAGLE® BRAND Sweetened Condensed Milk
  (NOT evaporated milk)
2 cups (12 ounces) semi-sweet chocolate chips*
1 cup (6 ounces) peanut butter-flavored chips*

Butterscotch-flavored chips or white chocolate chips may be substituted for the semi-sweet chocolate chips and/or peanut butter chips.

1. Preheat oven to 350°F (325°F for glass dish). In 13×9-inch baking pan, melt butter in oven.

2. Sprinkle crumbs evenly over butter; pour **Eagle Brand** evenly over crumbs. Top with remaining ingredients; press down firmly.

3. Bake 25 to 30 minutes or until lightly browned. Cool. Cut into bars. Store covered at room temperature.   *Makes 24 to 36 bars*

 *Helpful Hint*

> For perfectly cut bars, line the entire pan with a sheet of aluminum foil first. When the bars are baked and have cooled, lift up the edges of the foil to remove the bars from the pan. Cut into individual squares, rectangles, triangles or diamonds and peel off the foil.

Chocolate Chip Treasure Cookies

Prep Time: 15 minutes   **Bake Time:** 9 to 10 minutes

1½ cups graham cracker crumbs
½ cup all-purpose flour
2 teaspoons baking powder
1 (14-ounce) can EAGLE® BRAND Sweetened Condensed Milk
   (NOT evaporated milk)
½ cup (1 stick) butter or margarine, softened
1⅓ cups flaked coconut
1 (12-ounce) package semi-sweet chocolate chips
1 cup chopped walnuts

1. Preheat oven to 375°F. In small bowl, combine crumbs, flour and baking powder.

2. In large bowl, beat **Eagle Brand** and butter until smooth. Add crumb mixture; mix well. Stir in coconut, chips and walnuts.

3. Drop by rounded tablespoons onto ungreased cookie sheets. Bake 9 to 10 minutes or until lightly browned. Store loosely covered at room temperature.   *Makes about 3 dozen*

Foolproof Dark Chocolate Fudge

Prep Time: 10 minutes   Chill Time: 2 hours

> **3 cups (18 ounces) semi-sweet chocolate chips**
> **1 (14-ounce) can EAGLE® BRAND Sweetened Condensed Milk**
>   **(NOT evaporated milk)**
>   **Dash of salt**
> ½ **to 1 cup chopped nuts (optional)**
> 1½ **teaspoons vanilla extract**

1. Line 8- or 9-inch square pan with foil. Butter foil; set aside.

2. In heavy saucepan over low heat, melt chips with **Eagle Brand** and salt. Remove from heat; stir in nuts and vanilla. Spread evenly in prepared pan.

3. Chill 2 hours or until firm. Turn fudge onto cutting board; peel off foil and cut into squares. Store covered in refrigerator.

Makes about 2 pounds

Marshmallow Fudge: Stir in 2 tablespoons butter with vanilla. Substitute 2 cups miniature marshmallows for nuts. Proceed as directed above.

Foolproof Dark Chocolate Fudge

Magic Cookie Bars

Prep Time: 10 minutes   Bake Time: 25 minutes

½ cup (1 stick) butter or margarine
1½ cups graham cracker crumbs
1 (14-ounce) can EAGLE® BRAND Sweetened Condensed Milk
   (NOT evaporated milk)
2 cups (12 ounces) semi-sweet chocolate chips
1⅓ cups flaked coconut
1 cup chopped nuts

1. Preheat oven to 350°F (325°F for glass dish). In 13×9-inch baking pan, melt butter in oven.

2. Sprinkle crumbs over butter; pour **Eagle Brand** evenly over crumbs. Layer evenly with remaining ingredients; press down firmly.

3. Bake 25 minutes or until lightly browned. Cool. Chill if desired. Cut into bars. Store loosely covered at room temperature.

Makes 24 to 36 bars

7-Layer Magic Cookie Bars: Substitute 1 cup (6 ounces) butterscotch-flavored chips* for 1 cup semi-sweet chocolate chips and proceed as directed above.

Peanut butter-flavored chips or white chocolate chips may be substituted for butterscotch-flavored chips.

Magic Peanut Cookie Bars: Substitute 2 cups (about ¾ pound) chocolate-covered peanuts for semi-sweet chocolate chips and chopped nuts.

Magic Rainbow Cookie Bars: Substitute 2 cups plain candy-coated chocolate candies for semi-sweet chocolate chips.

Top to bottom: 7-Layer Magic Cookie Bars and Magic Rainbow Cookie Bars

Magic Make It Your Way Drop Cookies

Prep Time: 15 minutes   Bake Time: 8 to 10 minutes

   3 cups sifted all-purpose flour
   3 teaspoons baking powder
  ¾ teaspoon salt
  ¾ cup (1½ sticks) butter or margarine, softened
   2 eggs
   1 teaspoon vanilla extract
   1 (14-ounce) can EAGLE® BRAND Sweetened Condensed Milk
     (NOT evaporated milk)
   One "favorite" ingredient (see below)

1. Preheat oven to 350°F. Grease baking sheets; set aside. In large bowl, sift together dry ingredients. Stir in butter, eggs, vanilla and **Eagle Brand.** Fold in one of your "favorite" ingredients.

2. Drop by level teaspoonfuls, about 2 inches apart, onto prepared baking sheets. Bake 8 to 10 minutes or until edges are slightly browned. Remove at once from baking sheet. Cool. Store covered at room temperature.   *Makes about 4 dozen*

"Make it your way" with your favorite ingredient (pick one):
1 (6-ounce) package semi-sweet chocolate chips
1½ cups raisins
1½ cups corn flakes
1½ cups toasted shredded coconut

Top to bottom: Magic Make It Your Way
Drop Cookies and Versatile Cut-Out
Cookies (page 96)

Versatile Cut-Out Cookies

Prep Time: 15 minutes   Bake Time: 7 to 9 minutes

  3⅓ cups all-purpose flour
    1 tablespoon baking powder
    ½ teaspoon salt
    1 (14-ounce) can EAGLE® BRAND Sweetened Condensed Milk
        (NOT evaporated milk)
  ¾ cup (1½ sticks) butter or margarine, softened
    2 eggs
    2 teaspoons vanilla *or* 1½ teaspoons almond or lemon extract
        Ready-to-spread frosting

1. Preheat oven to 350°F. Grease baking sheets; set aside. In medium bowl, combine flour, baking powder and salt; set aside. In large bowl, beat **Eagle Brand,** butter, eggs and vanilla until well blended. Add dry ingredients; mix well.

2. On floured surface, lightly knead dough to form smooth ball. Divide into thirds. On well-floured surface, roll out each portion to ⅛-inch thickness. Cut with floured cookie cutter. Place 1 inch apart on prepared sheets.

3. Bake 7 to 9 minutes or until lightly browned around edges. Cool completely. Frost and decorate as desired. Store loosely covered at room temperature.   *Makes about 6½ dozen*

Sandwich Cookies: Use 2½-inch cookie cutter. Bake as directed above. Sandwich two cookies together with ready-to-spread frosting. Sprinkle with powdered sugar or colored sugar if desired. Makes about 3 dozen.

Festive Cranberry Cheese Bars

Prep Time: 25 minutes   **Bake Time:** 60 minutes

> 2 cups all-purpose flour
> 1½ cups oats
> 1 cup (2 sticks) butter or margarine, softened
> ¾ cup plus 1 tablespoon firmly packed brown sugar, divided
> 1 (8-ounce) package cream cheese, softened
> 1 (14-ounce) can EAGLE® BRAND Sweetened Condensed Milk
>   (NOT evaporated milk)
> ¼ cup REALEMON® Lemon Juice From Concentrate
> 1 (16-ounce) can whole berry cranberry sauce
> 2 tablespoons cornstarch

1. Preheat oven to 350°F. Grease 13×9-inch baking pan. In large bowl, beat flour, oats, butter and ¾ cup sugar until crumbly. Reserve 1½ cups crumb mixture. Press remaining crumb mixture on bottom of prepared pan. Bake 15 minutes or until lightly browned.

2. Meanwhile, in medium bowl, beat cream cheese until fluffy. Gradually beat in **Eagle Brand** until smooth; stir in **ReaLemon**. Spread over baked crust. Combine cranberry sauce, cornstarch and remaining 1 tablespoon sugar. Spoon over cheese layer. Top with reserved crumb mixture.

3. Bake 45 minutes or until golden. Cool and cut into bars. Store covered in refrigerator.   *Makes 24 to 36 bars*

Tip: Cut into large squares. Serve warm and top with ice cream.

Cheesecake-Topped Brownies

Prep Time: 20 minutes   **Bake Time:** 40 to 45 minutes

> 1 (21- or 23.6-ounce) package fudge brownie mix
> 1 (8-ounce) package cream cheese, softened
> 2 tablespoons butter or margarine, softened
> 1 tablespoon cornstarch
> 1 (14-ounce) can EAGLE® BRAND Sweetened Condensed Milk
>   (NOT evaporated milk)
> 1 egg
> 2 teaspoons vanilla extract
>   Ready-to-spread chocolate frosting (optional)
>   Orange peel (optional)

1. Preheat oven to 350°F. Prepare brownie mix as package directs. Spread into well-greased 13×9-inch baking pan.

2. In large mixing bowl, beat cream cheese, butter and cornstarch until fluffy.

3. Gradually beat in **Eagle Brand**. Add egg and vanilla; beat until smooth. Pour cheesecake mixture evenly over brownie batter.

4. Bake 40 to 45 minutes or until top is lightly browned. Cool. Spread with frosting or sprinkle with orange peel, if desired. Cut into bars. Store covered in refrigerator.   *Makes 36 to 40 bars*

Cheesecake-Topped Brownies

Lemon Crumb Bars

Prep Time: 30 minutes   Bake Time: 35 minutes

1 (18¼-ounce) package lemon or yellow cake mix
½ cup (1 stick) butter or margarine, softened
1 egg plus 3 egg yolks
2 cups finely crushed saltine crackers (¼ pound)
1 (14-ounce) can EAGLE® BRAND Sweetened Condensed Milk
    (NOT evaporated milk)
½ cup REALEMON® Lemon Juice from Concentrate

1. Preheat oven to 350°F. Grease 15×10×1-inch baking pan. In large bowl, combine cake mix, butter and 1 egg; mix well (mixture will be crumbly). Stir in cracker crumbs. Reserve 2 cups crumb mixture. Press remaining crumb mixture firmly on bottom of prepared pan. Bake 15 minutes.

2. Meanwhile, in medium bowl, combine egg yolks, **Eagle Brand** and **ReaLemon;** mix well. Spread evenly over baked crust.

3. Top with reserved crumb mixture. Bake 20 minutes or until firm. Cool. Cut into bars. Store covered in refrigerator.

Makes 36 to 48 bars

 *Helpful Hint*

Here's a quick and easy way to make cracker or cookie crumbs: place crackers in a large resealable plastic food storage bag; seal. Roll a rolling pin over the crackers to crush.

Lemon Crumb Bars

Fast 'n' Fabulous

*U*nexpected company dropping by? A merry group of little elves suddenly appearing on your doorstep? No problem! Any time you need a treat in a hurry you can whip up one of the delicious bars, outstanding cookies or wonderful treats in this chapter. And you can prepare these desserts in just 15 minutes or less! Eagle® Brand treats taste great, are easy to make, and are sure to satisfy all your guests. So fast and fabulous you'll think they're magic. Be careful. Your guests may never want to leave.

102

S'Mores on a Stick (page 104)

S'Mores on a Stick

Prep Time: 10 minutes   **Cook Time:** 3 minutes

**1 (14-ounce) can EAGLE® BRAND Sweetened Condensed Milk
(NOT evaporated milk)**
1½ cups milk chocolate mini chips, divided
1 cup miniature marshmallows
11 whole graham crackers, halved crosswise
**Toppings chopped peanuts, candy-coated chocolate mini
pieces, sprinkles**

1. Microwave half of **Eagle Brand** in microwave-safe bowl on HIGH (100% power) 1½ minutes. Stir in 1 cup chocolate chips until smooth; stir in marshmallows.

2. Spread evenly by heaping tablespoonfuls onto 11 graham cracker halves. Top with remaining graham cracker halves; place on waxed paper.

3. Microwave remaining **Eagle Brand** at HIGH (100% power) 1½ minutes; stir in remaining ½ cup chocolate chips, stirring until smooth. Drizzle mixture over cookies and sprinkle with desired toppings.

4. Let stand for 2 hours; insert a wooden craft stick in center of each cookie. *Makes 11 servings*

Coconut Macaroons

Prep Time: 10 minutes   **Bake Time:** 15 to 17 minutes

> **1 (14-ounce) can EAGLE® BRAND Sweetened Condensed Milk**
> **(NOT evaporated milk)**
> **2 teaspoons vanilla extract**
> **1 to 1½ teaspoons almond extract**
> **2 (7-ounce) packages flaked coconut (5⅓ cups)**

1. Preheat oven to 325°F. Line baking sheets with foil; grease and flour foil. Set aside.

2. In large bowl, combine **Eagle Brand,** vanilla and almond extract. Stir in coconut. Drop by rounded teaspoons onto prepared sheets; with spoon, slightly flatten each mound.

3. Bake 15 to 17 minutes or until golden. Remove from baking sheets; cool on wire racks. Store loosely covered at room temperature.

Makes about 4 dozen

 *Helpful Hint*

> *If you want to trim the fat in any Eagle® Brand recipe, just use Eagle® Brand Fat Free or Low Fat Sweetened Condensed Milk instead of the original Eagle® Brand.*

White Chocolate Squares

Prep Time: 15 minutes   Bake Time: 20 to 25 minutes

> 1 (12-ounce) package white chocolate chips, divided
> ¼ cup (½ stick) butter or margarine
> 2 cups all-purpose flour
> ½ teaspoon baking powder
> 1 (14-ounce) can EAGLE® BRAND Sweetened Condensed Milk
>   (NOT evaporated milk)
> 1 cup chopped pecans, toasted
> 1 large egg
> 1 teaspoon vanilla extract
>   Powdered sugar

1. Preheat oven to 350°F. Grease 13×9-inch baking pan. In large saucepan over low heat, melt 1 cup chips and butter. Stir in flour and baking powder until blended. Stir in **Eagle Brand,** pecans, egg, vanilla and remaining chips. Spoon mixture into prepared pan.

2. Bake 20 to 25 minutes. Cool. Sprinkle with powdered sugar; cut into squares. Store covered at room temperature.   *Makes 24 bars*

 *Helpful Hint*

> *Toasted nuts and coconut give foods a pleasant crunchiness and enhance the food's nutty flavor. To toast, spread the chopped nuts or coconut in a single layer in a shallow baking pan. Preheat the oven to 350°F. Bake 5 to 10 minutes or until light golden brown, stirring frequently to prevent burning.*

White Chocolate Squares

Cookie Pizza

Prep Time: 15 minutes   Bake Time: 14 minutes

1 (18-ounce) package refrigerated sugar cookie dough
2 cups (12 ounces) semi-sweet chocolate chips
1 (14-ounce) can EAGLE® BRAND Sweetened Condensed Milk
   (NOT evaporated milk)
2 cups candy-coated milk chocolate candies
2 cups miniature marshmallows
½ cup peanuts

1. Preheat oven to 375°F. Press cookie dough into 2 ungreased 12-inch pizza pans. Bake 10 minutes or until golden. Remove from oven.

2. In medium-sized saucepan, melt chips with **Eagle Brand.** Spread over crusts. Sprinkle with milk chocolate candies, marshmallows and peanuts.

3. Bake 4 minutes or until marshmallows are lightly toasted. Cool. Cut into wedges.   *Makes 2 pizzas (24 servings)*

Cookie Pizza

Chocolate, Chocolate, Chocolate

Aahh, the sweet indulgence of rich, creamy chocolate. For anyone with a true passion for chocolate, the very mention of the word can cause shivers of delight and anticipation. Let your chocolate dreams come true with Eagle® Brand, the magic ingredient for foolproof, richly satisfying bars and cookies or melt-in-your-mouth confections. These and other Eagle® Brand recipes found in this chapter are sure to send any chocoholic to chocolate heaven!

110

Top to bottom: Double Chocolate Brownies (page 112) and Rocky Road Candy (page 113)

Double Chocolate Brownies

Prep Time: 15 minutes   **Bake Time:** 35 minutes

 1¼ cups all-purpose flour, divided
 ¼ cup sugar
 ½ cup (1 stick) cold butter or margarine
 1 (14-ounce) can EAGLE® BRAND Sweetened Condensed Milk
     (NOT evaporated milk)
 ¼ cup unsweetened cocoa
 1 egg
 1 teaspoon vanilla extract
 ½ teaspoon baking powder
 1 (8-ounce) milk chocolate bar, broken into chunks
 ¾ cup chopped nuts (optional)

1. Preheat oven to 350°F. Line 13×9-inch baking pan with foil; set aside.

2. In medium bowl, combine 1 cup flour and sugar; cut in butter until crumbly. Press firmly on bottom of prepared pan. Bake 15 minutes.

3. In large bowl, beat **Eagle Brand,** cocoa, egg, remaining ¼ cup flour, vanilla and baking powder. Stir in chocolate chunks and nuts. Spread over baked crust. Bake 20 minutes or until set.

4. Cool. Use foil to lift out of pan. Cut into bars. Store tightly covered at room temperature.   *Makes 24 brownies*

Rocky Road Candy

Prep Time: 10 minutes   **Chill Time:** 2 hours

> 1 (12-ounce) package semi-sweet chocolate chips
> 2 tablespoons butter or margarine
> 1 (14-ounce) can EAGLE® BRAND Sweetened Condensed Milk
>   (NOT evaporated milk)
> 2 cups dry roasted peanuts
> 1 (10½-ounce) package miniature marshmallows

1. Line 13×9-inch baking pan with waxed paper. In heavy saucepan over low heat, melt chips and butter with **Eagle Brand;** remove from heat.

2. In large bowl, combine peanuts and marshmallows; stir in chocolate mixture. Spread in prepared pan. Chill 2 hours or until firm.

3. Remove candy from pan; peel off paper and cut into squares. Store loosely covered at room temperature.

Makes about 3½ dozen

Microwave Directions: In 1-quart glass measure, combine chips, butter and **Eagle Brand.** Microwave on HIGH (100% power) 3 minutes, stirring after 1½ minutes. Stir to melt chips. Let stand 5 minutes. Proceed as directed above.

 *Helpful Hint*

For a more festive look, try cutting bars and candies into different shapes, such as rectangles, triangles or diamonds. To make diamonds, cut straight lines 1 to 1½ inches apart down the length of the bars. Then, diagonally cut straight lines 1 to 1½ inches apart across the bars.

Chocolate Peanut Butter Chip Cookies

Prep Time: 15 minutes   **Bake Time:** 6 to 8 minutes

8 (1-ounce) squares semi-sweet chocolate
3 tablespoons margarine or butter
1 (14-ounce) can EAGLE® BRAND Sweetened Condensed Milk
    (NOT evaporated milk)
2 cups biscuit baking mix
1 teaspoon vanilla extract
1 cup (6-ounces) peanut butter-flavored chips

1. Preheat oven to 350°F. In large saucepan, over low heat, melt chocolate and butter with **Eagle Brand;** remove from heat. Add biscuit mix and vanilla; with mixer, beat until smooth and well blended.

2. Cool to room temperature. Stir in chips. Shape into 1¼-inch balls. Place 2 inches apart on ungreased baking sheets. Bake 6 to 8 minutes or until tops are slightly crusted. Cool. Store tightly covered at room temperature.   *Makes about 4 dozen*

Chocolate Peanut Butter Chip Cookies

No-Bake Fudgy Brownies

Prep Time: 10 minutes   Chill Time: 4 hours

> 1 (14-ounce) can EAGLE® BRAND Sweetened Condensed Milk (NOT evaporated milk)
> 2 (1-ounce) squares unsweetened chocolate, cut up
> 1 teaspoon vanilla extract
> 2 cups plus 2 tablespoons packaged chocolate cookie crumbs
> ¼ cup miniature candy-coated milk chocolate candies or chopped nuts

1. Grease 8-inch square baking pan or line with foil; set aside.

2. In medium-sized heavy saucepan, combine **Eagle Brand** and chocolate; cook and stir over low heat just until boiling. Reduce heat; cook and stir for 2 to 3 minutes more or until mixture thickens. Remove from heat. Stir in vanilla.

3. Stir in 2 cups cookie crumbs. Spread evenly in prepared pan. Sprinkle with remaining cookie crumbs and candies or nuts; press down gently with back of spoon.

4. Cover and chill 4 hours or until firm. Cut into squares. Store covered in refrigerator.   *Makes 24 to 36 bars*

No-Bake Fudgy Brownies

Double Chocolate Cookies

Prep Time: 15 minutes   **Bake Time:** 10 minutes

> **2 cups biscuit baking mix**
> **1 (14-ounce) can EAGLE® BRAND Sweetened Condensed Milk (NOT evaporated milk)**
> **8 (1-ounce) squares semi-sweet chocolate** *or* **1 (12-ounce) package semi-sweet chocolate chips, melted**
> **3 tablespoons butter or margarine, melted**
> **1 egg**
> **1 teaspoon vanilla extract**
> **6 (1¼-ounce) white candy bars with almonds, broken into small pieces**
> **¾ cup chopped nuts**

1. Preheat oven to 350°F. In large bowl, combine all ingredients except candy pieces and nuts; beat until smooth.

2. Stir in remaining ingredients. Drop by rounded teaspoonfuls, 2 inches apart, onto ungreased baking sheets.

3. Bake 10 minutes or until tops are slightly crusted (do not overbake). Cool. Store tightly covered at room temperature.

Makes about 4½ dozen

Mint Chocolate Cookies: Substitute ¾ cup mint-flavored chocolate chips for white candy bars with almonds. Proceed as directed above.

Top to bottom: Double Chocolate Cookies and Chocolate Raspberry Truffles (page 120)

Chocolate Raspberry Truffles

Prep Time: 10 minutes   **Cook Time:** 3 minutes
Chill Time: 1 hour

> **1 (14-ounce) can EAGLE® BRAND Sweetened Condensed Milk
>   (NOT evaporated milk)**
> **¼ cup raspberry liqueur**
> **2 tablespoons butter or margarine**
> **2 tablespoons seedless raspberry jam**
> **2 (12-ounce) packages semi-sweet chocolate chips**
> **½ cup powdered sugar or ground toasted almonds**

1. Microwave first 4 ingredients in large microwave-safe bowl on
HIGH (100% power) 3 minutes.

2. Stir in chips until smooth. Cover and chill 1 hour.

3. Shape mixture into 1-inch balls and roll in powdered sugar or
almonds. Store covered at room temperature.   *Makes 4 dozen*

 *Helpful Hint*

> *Use your food processor to easily grind the toasted almonds in this recipe.*
> *Be careful not to overprocess the nuts, however. If they are overprocessed,*
> *nuts will become nut butter.*

Buckeye Cookie Bars

Prep Time: 20 minutes   Bake Time: 25 to 30 minutes

   1 (18¼-ounce) package chocolate cake mix
¼ cup vegetable oil
   1 egg
   1 cup chopped peanuts
   1 (14-ounce) can EAGLE® BRAND Sweetened Condensed Milk
      (NOT evaporated milk)
½ cup peanut butter

1. Preheat oven to 350°F.

2. In large mixing bowl, combine cake mix, oil and egg; beat on medium speed until crumbly. Stir in peanuts. Reserving 1½ cups crumb mixture, press remainder firmly on bottom of greased 13×9-inch baking pan.

3. In medium bowl, beat **Eagle Brand** with peanut butter until smooth; spread over prepared crust. Sprinkle with reserved crumb mixture.

4. Bake 25 to 30 minutes or until set. Cool. Cut into bars. Store loosely covered at room temperature.   *Makes 24 to 36 bars*

Fudge-Filled Bars

Prep Time: 20 minutes   Bake Time: 25 to 30 minutes

1 (14-ounce) can EAGLE® BRAND Sweetened Condensed Milk (NOT evaporated milk)
1 (12-ounce) package semi-sweet chocolate chips
2 tablespoons butter or margarine
2 teaspoons vanilla extract
2 (18-ounce) packages refrigerated cookie dough (oatmeal-chocolate chip, chocolate chip, or sugar cookie dough)

1. Preheat oven to 350°F. In heavy saucepan over medium heat, combine **Eagle Brand,** chips and butter; heat until chips melt, stirring often. Remove from heat; stir in vanilla. Cool 15 minutes.

2. Using floured hands, press 1½ packages of cookie dough into ungreased 15×10×1-inch baking pan. Pour cooled chocolate mixture evenly over dough. Crumble remaining dough over filling.

3. Bake 25 to 30 minutes. Cool. Cut into bars. Store covered at room temperature.
Makes 48 bars

Fudge-Filled Bars

Any-Day Delights

Scrumptious bars and brownies, crispy cookies or rich fudge are just the thing to turn a ho-hum day into a delight. You will see nothing but smiles when they know that you've made delicious Eagle® Brand treats. Eagle® Brand transforms simple ingredients you keep on hand into extra-special treats. And these goodies are so simple to make, you won't want to wait for a special occasion. So make any day brighter with the magic of Eagle® Brand.

Clockwise from top right: Peanut Blossom Cookies (page 126), Easy Peanut Butter Cookies (page 126) and Crunchy Clusters (page 127)

124

Easy Peanut Butter Cookies

Prep Time: 10 minutes   **Chill Time:** 1 hour
Bake Time: 6 to 8 minutes

> 1 (14-ounce) can EAGLE® BRAND Sweetened Condensed Milk
>   (NOT evaporated milk)
> ¾ to 1 cup peanut butter
> 1 egg
> 1 teaspoon vanilla extract
> 2 cups biscuit baking mix
>   Sugar

1. In large bowl, beat **Eagle Brand,** peanut butter, egg and vanilla until smooth. Add biscuit mix; mix well. Chill at least 1 hour.

2. Preheat oven to 350°F. Shape dough into 1-inch balls. Roll in sugar. Place 2 inches apart on ungreased baking sheets.

3. Flatten with fork in criss-cross pattern. Bake 6 to 8 minutes or until lightly browned (do not overbake). Cool. Store tightly covered at room temperature.   *Makes about 5 dozen*

Peanut Blossom Cookies: Make dough as directed above. Shape into 1-inch balls and roll in sugar; do not flatten. Bake as directed above. Immediately after baking, press solid milk chocolate candy drop in center of each cookie.

Peanut Butter & Jelly Gems: Make dough as directed above. Shape into 1-inch balls and roll in sugar; do not flatten. Press thumb in center of each ball of dough; fill with jelly, jam or preserves. Proceed as directed above.

Any-Way-You-Like 'em Cookies: Stir 1 cup semi-sweet chocolate chips, chopped peanuts, raisins or flaked coconut into dough. Proceed as directed above.

Crunchy Clusters

Prep Time: 10 minutes   **Chill Time:** 2 hours

1 (12-ounce) package semi-sweet chocolate chips *or* 3 (6-ounce) packages butterscotch-flavored chips
1 (14-ounce) can EAGLE® BRAND Sweetened Condensed Milk (NOT evaporated milk)
1 (3-ounce) can chow mein noodles *or* 2 cups pretzel sticks, broken into ½-inch pieces
1 cup dry-roasted peanuts or whole roasted almonds

1. Line baking sheet with waxed paper. In heavy saucepan over low heat, melt chips with **Eagle Brand.** Remove from heat.

2. In large bowl, combine noodles and peanuts; stir in chocolate mixture.

3. Drop by tablespoonfuls onto prepared baking sheet; chill 2 hours or until firm. Store loosely covered at room temperature.

Makes about 3 dozen

Microwave Directions: In 2-quart glass measure, combine chips and **Eagle Brand.** Microwave on HIGH (100% power) 3 minutes, stirring after 1½ minutes. Stir until smooth. Proceed as directed above.

 *Helpful Hint*

> *Here are some other ways to make any day special with Eagle® Brand:*
> - *Offer it as a topper for waffles and French toast.*
> - *Pour it directly into a pretty bowl for a fruit dip.*
> - *Spoon some over cake instead of frosting.*
> - *Stir it into coffee or tea for a coffeehouse-type beverage.*

Golden Peanut Butter Bars

Prep Time: 20 minutes   **Bake Time:** 40 minutes

   2 cups all-purpose flour
   ¾ cup firmly packed light brown sugar
   1 egg, beaten
   ½ cup (1 stick) cold butter or margarine
   1 cup finely chopped peanuts
   1 (14-ounce) can EAGLE® BRAND Sweetened Condensed Milk
      (NOT evaporated milk)
   ½ cup peanut butter
   1 teaspoon vanilla extract

1. Preheat oven to 350°F. Combine flour, sugar and egg in large bowl; cut in cold butter until crumbly. Stir in peanuts. Reserve 2 cups crumb mixture. Press remaining mixture on bottom of 13×9-inch baking pan.

2. Bake 15 minutes or until lightly browned.

3. Meanwhile, beat **Eagle Brand,** peanut butter and vanilla in another large bowl. Spread over prepared crust; top with reserved crumb mixture.

4. Bake an additional 25 minutes or until lightly browned. Cool. Cut into bars. Store covered at room temperature.   *Makes 24 to 36 bars*

Golden Peanut Butter Bars

Double Chocolate Fantasy Bars

Prep Time: 15 minutes   **Bake Time:** 25 to 30 minutes

1 (18¼-ounce) package chocolate cake mix
¼ cup vegetable oil
1 egg
1 cup chopped nuts
1 (14-ounce) can EAGLE® BRAND Sweetened Condensed Milk
    (NOT evaporated milk)
1 (6-ounce) package semi-sweet chocolate chips
1 teaspoon vanilla extract
    Dash salt

1. Preheat oven to 350°F. Grease 13×9-inch baking pan. In large bowl, combine cake mix, oil and egg; beat on medium speed until crumbly. Stir in nuts. Reserve 1½ cups crumb mixture. Press remaining crumb mixture on bottom of prepared pan.

2. In small saucepan over medium heat, combine remaining ingredients. Cook and stir until chips melt.

3. Pour chocolate mixture evenly over prepared crust. Sprinkle reserved crumb mixture evenly over top. Bake 25 to 30 minutes or until set. Cool. Cut into bars. Store loosely covered at room temperature.
                                                            Makes 36 bars

*Top to bottom: Double Chocolate Fantasy
Bars and Toffee Bars (page 132)*

Toffee Bars

Prep Time: 45 minutes   Bake Time: 20 to 30 minutes

Cook Time: 15 minutes

    1 cup oats
   ½ cup packed brown sugar
   ½ cup all-purpose flour
   ½ cup finely chopped walnuts
   ½ cup (1 stick) butter or margarine, melted and divided
   ¼ teaspoon baking soda
    1 (14-ounce) can EAGLE® BRAND Sweetened Condensed Milk
       (NOT evaporated milk)
    2 teaspoons vanilla extract
    1 (6-ounce) package semi-sweet chocolate chips

1. Preheat oven to 350°F. Grease 13×9-inch baking pan. Combine oats, sugar, flour, walnuts, 6 tablespoons butter and baking soda. Press firmly on bottom of prepared pan. Bake 10 to 15 minutes or until lightly browned.

2. Meanwhile, in medium saucepan over medium heat, combine remaining 2 tablespoons butter and **Eagle Brand.** Cook and stir until mixture thickens slightly, about 15 minutes. Remove from heat; stir in vanilla. Pour over baked crust.

3. Bake 10 to 15 minutes or until golden brown.

4. Remove from oven; immediately sprinkle chips on top. Let stand 1 minute; spread chips while still warm. Cool. Cut into bars. Store tightly covered at room temperature.   *Makes 36 bars*

Quick No-Bake Brownies

Prep Time: 15 minutes   Chill Time: 4 hours

    1 cup finely chopped nuts, divided
    2 (1-ounce) squares unsweetened chocolate
    1 (14-ounce) can EAGLE® BRAND Sweetened Condensed Milk
       (NOT evaporated milk)
    2 to 2½ cups vanilla wafer crumbs (about 48 to 60 wafers)

1. Grease 9-inch square pan with butter. Sprinkle ¼ cup nuts evenly in bottom of pan. In heavy saucepan over low heat, melt chocolate with **Eagle Brand.** Cook and stir until mixture thickens, about 10 minutes.

2. Remove from heat; stir in crumbs and ½ cup nuts. Spread evenly in prepared pan.

3. Top with remaining ¼ cup nuts. Chill 4 hours or until firm. Cut into squares. Store loosely covered at room temperature.

Makes 24 brownies

Butterscotch Apple Squares

Prep Time: 15 minutes   **Bake Time:** 25 to 30 minutes

   ¼ **cup (½ stick) butter or margarine**
1½ **cups graham cracker crumbs**
   2 **small all-purpose apples, pared and chopped (about 1¼ cups)**
   1 **(6-ounce) package butterscotch-flavored chips**
   1 **(14-ounce) can EAGLE® BRAND Sweetened Condensed Milk (NOT evaporated milk)**
 1⅓ **cups flaked coconut**
   1 **cup chopped nuts**

1. Preheat oven to 350°F (325°F for glass dish). In 13×9-inch baking pan, melt butter in oven. Sprinkle crumbs evenly over butter; top with apples.

2. In heavy saucepan over medium heat, melt chips with **Eagle Brand.** Pour butterscotch mixture evenly over apples. Top with coconut and nuts; press down firmly.

3. Bake 25 to 30 minutes or until lightly browned. Cool. Cut into squares. Store covered in refrigerator.   *Makes 12 servings*

Cookies 'n' Crème Fudge

Prep Time: 10 minutes   Chill Time: 2 hours

3 (6-ounce) packages white chocolate baking squares
1 (14-ounce) can EAGLE® BRAND Sweetened Condensed Milk
  (NOT evaporated milk)
⅛ teaspoon salt
2 cups coarsely crushed chocolate crème-filled sandwich cookies
  (about 20 cookies)

1. Line 8-inch square baking pan with foil. In heavy saucepan over low heat, melt chocolate with **Eagle Brand** and salt. Remove from heat. Stir in crushed cookies. Spread evenly in prepared pan. Chill 2 hours or until firm.

2. Turn fudge onto cutting board. Peel off foil; cut into squares. Store tightly covered at room temperature.   *Makes about 2½ pounds*

No-Bake Peanutty Chocolate Drops

Prep Time: 10 minutes   Chill Time: 2 hours

½ cup (1 stick) butter or margarine
⅓ cup unsweetened cocoa
1 (14-ounce) can EAGLE® BRAND Sweetened Condensed Milk
  (NOT evaporated milk)
2½ cups quick-cooking oats
1 cup chopped peanuts
½ cup peanut butter

1. Line baking sheets with waxed paper. In medium saucepan over medium heat, melt butter; stir in cocoa. Bring mixture to a boil.

2. Remove from heat; stir in remaining ingredients.

3. Drop by teaspoonfuls onto prepared baking sheets; chill 2 hours or until set. Store loosely covered in refrigerator.

Makes about 5 dozen

Cookies 'n' Crème Fudge

Candy Bar Bars

Prep Time: 20 minutes   Bake Time: 40 minutes

¾ cup (1½ sticks) butter or margarine, softened
¼ cup peanut butter
1 cup packed brown sugar
1 teaspoon baking soda
2 cups quick-cooking oats
1½ cups all-purpose flour
1 egg
1 (14-ounce) can EAGLE® BRAND Sweetened Condensed Milk
    (NOT evaporated milk)
4 cups chopped candy bars (such as chocolate-coated caramel-
    topped nougat bars with peanuts, chocolate-covered crisp
    wafers, chocolate-covered caramel-topped cookie bars, or
    chocolate-covered peanut butter cups)

1. Preheat oven to 350°F. In large bowl, combine butter and peanut butter. Add sugar and baking soda; beat well. Stir in oats and flour. Reserve 1¾ cups crumb mixture.

2. Stir egg into remaining crumb mixture; press firmly on bottom of ungreased 15×10×1-inch baking pan. Bake 15 minutes.

3. Spread **Eagle Brand** over baked crust. Stir together reserved crumb mixture and candy bar pieces; sprinkle evenly over top. Bake 25 minutes or until golden. Cool. Cut into bars. Store covered at room temperature. *Makes 48 bars*

Candy Bar Bars

Luscious Homemade Gifts

What better way to show you care than to make a mouth-watering goodie that everyone can enjoy. Whether it's to say "Happy Holidays," "Welcome to the Neighborhood" or "Thank You," nothing says it sweeter and easier than these magical cookies, incredible bars and festive candies. Best of all, because these sweets are made with Eagle® Brand and made by you, they're the best gift you can give. Eagle® Brand makes "homemade"…magic.

Top to bottom: Chocolate Pecan Critters (page 140), Peanut Butter Fudge (page 140) and Layered Mint Chocolate Candy (page 141)

Chocolate Pecan Critters

Prep Time: 10 minutes

    1 (11½-ounce) package milk chocolate chips
    1 (6-ounce) package semi-sweet chocolate chips
    ¼ cup (½ stick) butter or margarine
    1 (14-ounce) can EAGLE® BRAND Sweetened Condensed Milk
       (NOT evaporated milk)
    ⅛ teaspoon salt
    2 cups coarsely chopped pecans
    2 teaspoons vanilla extract
      Pecan halves

1. Line baking sheets with waxed paper. In heavy saucepan over medium heat, melt chips and butter with **Eagle Brand** and salt.

2. Remove from heat; stir in chopped pecans and vanilla.

3. Drop by spoonfuls onto prepared baking sheets. Top with pecan halves. Chill. Store tightly covered at room temperature.

Makes about 5 dozen

Microwave Directions: In 2-quart glass measure, microwave chips, butter, **Eagle Brand** and salt on HIGH (100% power) 3 minutes. Stir after 1½ minutes. Stir to melt chips; add chopped pecans and vanilla. Proceed as directed above.

Peanut Butter Fudge

Prep Time: 5 minutes   Cook Time: 4 to 5 minutes
Chill Time: 2 hours

    2 (10-ounce) packages peanut butter-flavored chips
    1 (14-ounce) can EAGLE® BRAND Sweetened Condensed Milk
       (NOT evaporated milk)
    ¼ cup (½ stick) butter or margarine, cut into pieces
    1 cup chopped salted peanuts

1. Butter 8-inch square dish. Microwave first 3 ingredients in a 2-quart microwave-safe bowl on MEDIUM (50% power) 4 to 5 minutes, stirring at 1½-minute intervals.

2. Stir in peanuts and pour into prepared dish. Cover and chill 2 hours. Cut into squares. Store covered in refrigerator.

Makes 2 pounds

Layered Mint Chocolate Candy

Prep Time: 20 minutes   Chill Time: 2 hours 20 minutes

> 1 (12-ounce) package semi-sweet chocolate chips
> 1 (14-ounce) can EAGLE® BRAND Sweetened Condensed Milk
>   (NOT evaporated milk), divided
> 2 teaspoons vanilla extract
> 1 cup (6 ounces) deluxe white baking chips
> 1 tablespoon peppermint extract
>   Few drops green or red food coloring (optional)

1. Line 8- or 9-inch square pan with waxed paper. In heavy saucepan over low heat, melt semi-sweet chips with 1 cup **Eagle Brand.** Stir in vanilla. Spread half the mixture in prepared pan; chill 10 minutes or until firm. Keep remaining chocolate mixture at room temperature.

2. In heavy saucepan over low heat, melt white chips with remaining **Eagle Brand.** Stir in peppermint extract and food coloring. Spread over chilled chocolate layer; chill 10 minutes or until firm. Spread reserved chocolate mixture over mint layer. Chill 2 hours or until firm.

3. Turn candy onto cutting board; peel off paper and cut into squares. Store loosely covered at room temperature.

Makes about 1¾ pounds

Choco-Peanut Pinwheels

Prep Time: 15 minutes   Chill Time: 2 hours

1 cup (6 ounces) peanut butter-flavored chips
1 (14-ounce) can EAGLE® BRAND Sweetened Condensed Milk
    (NOT evaporated milk)
1 cup (6 ounces) semi-sweet chocolate chips
1 teaspoon vanilla extract

1. Cut waxed paper into 15×10-inch rectangle; butter paper.

2. In heavy saucepan, over low heat, melt peanut butter chips with ⅔ cup **Eagle Brand.** Cool slightly. With fingers, press evenly into thin layer to cover waxed paper. Let stand at room temperature 15 minutes.

3. In heavy saucepan, melt chocolate chips with remaining **Eagle Brand.** Remove from heat; stir in vanilla. Spread evenly over peanut butter layer. Let stand at room temperature 30 minutes.

4. Beginning at 15-inch side, roll up tightly, jelly roll-fashion, without waxed paper. Wrap tightly in plastic wrap.

5. Chill 2 hours or until firm. Cut into ¼-inch slices to serve. Store covered at room temperature.   *Makes about 1½ pounds*

Double Chocolate Cherry Cookies

Prep Time: 25 minutes   **Bake Time:** 8 to 10 minutes

1¼ cups (2½ sticks) butter or margarine, softened
1¾ cups sugar
2 eggs
1 tablespoon vanilla extract
3½ cups all-purpose flour
¾ cup unsweetened cocoa
½ teaspoon baking powder
½ teaspoon baking soda
¼ teaspoon salt
2 (6-ounce) jars maraschino cherries, well drained and halved
    (about 60 cherries)
1 (6-ounce) package semi-sweet chocolate chips
1 (14-ounce) can EAGLE® BRAND Sweetened Condensed Milk
    (NOT evaporated milk)

1. Preheat oven to 350°F. In large bowl, beat butter and sugar until fluffy. Add eggs and vanilla; mix well.

2. In large bowl, combine dry ingredients; stir into butter mixture (dough will be stiff). Shape into 1-inch balls. Place 1 inch apart on ungreased baking sheets.

3. Press cherry half into center of each cookie. Bake 8 to 10 minutes. Cool.

4. In heavy saucepan over medium heat, melt chips with **Eagle Brand;** cook until mixture thickens, about 3 minutes. Frost each cookie, covering cherry. Store loosely covered at room temperature.
Makes about 10 dozen

Double Chocolate Pecan Cookies: Prepare and shape dough as directed above, omitting cherries. Flatten. Bake and frost as directed. Garnish each cookie with pecan half.

Easy Chocolate Truffles

Prep Time: 10 minutes   Chill Time: 3 hours

3 (6-ounce) packages semi-sweet chocolate chips
1 (14-ounce) can EAGLE® BRAND Sweetened Condensed Milk
**   (NOT evaporated milk)**
1 tablespoon vanilla extract
**   Coatings: finely chopped nuts, flaked coconut, chocolate**
**   sprinkles, colored sprinkles, unsweetened cocoa or colored**
**   sugar**

1. In heavy saucepan over low heat, melt chips with **Eagle Brand.** Remove from heat; stir in vanilla.

2. Chill 2 hours or until firm. Shape into 1-inch balls; roll in desired coating.

3. Chill 1 hour or until firm. Store covered at room temperature.

Makes about 6 dozen

Microwave Directions: In 1-quart measure, combine chips and **Eagle Brand.** Cook on HIGH (100% power) 3 minutes, stirring after 1½ minutes. Stir until smooth. Proceed as directed above.

Amaretto Truffles: Substitute 3 tablespoons amaretto liqueur and ½ teaspoon almond extract for vanilla. Roll in finely chopped toasted almonds.

Orange Truffles: Substitute 3 tablespoons orange-flavored liqueur for vanilla. Roll in finely chopped toasted almonds mixed with finely grated orange rind.

Rum Truffles: Substitute ¼ cup dark rum for vanilla. Roll in flaked coconut.

Bourbon Truffles: Substitute 3 tablespoons bourbon for vanilla. Roll in finely chopped toasted nuts.

Peppermint Chocolate Fudge

Prep Time: 10 minutes   Chill Time: 2 hours

> 1 (12-ounce) package milk chocolate chips (2 cups)
> 1 cup (6 ounces) semi-sweet chocolate chips
> 1 (14-ounce) can EAGLE® BRAND Sweetened Condensed Milk (NOT evaporated milk)
>   Dash salt
> ½ teaspoon peppermint extract
> ¼ cup crushed hard peppermint candy

1. In saucepan, over low heat, melt chips with **Eagle Brand** and salt. Remove from heat; stir in extract. Spread evenly into foil-lined 8- or 9-inch square pan. Sprinkle with peppermint candy.

2. Chill 2 hours or until firm. Turn fudge onto cutting board; peel off foil and cut into squares. Store loosely covered at room temperature.

Makes about 2 pounds

Chocolate Snowswirl Fudge

Prep Time: 10 minutes

> 3 cups (18 ounces) semi-sweet chocolate chips
> 1 (14-ounce) can EAGLE® BRAND Sweetened Condensed Milk (NOT evaporated milk)
> 4 tablespoons butter or margarine, divided
> 1½ teaspoons vanilla extract
>   Dash salt
> 1 cup chopped nuts
> 2 cups miniature marshmallows

1. Melt chips with **Eagle Brand,** 2 tablespoons butter, vanilla and salt. Remove from heat; stir in nuts. Spread evenly into foil-lined 8- or 9-inch square pan.

2. Melt marshmallows with remaining 2 tablespoons butter. Spread on top of fudge. With table knife or metal spatula, swirl through top of fudge.

3. Chill at least 2 hours or until firm. Turn fudge onto cutting board; peel off foil and cut into squares. Store loosely covered at room temperature.

Makes about 2 pounds

Peppermint Chocolate Fudge and
Chocolate Snowswirl Fudge

Chocolate Streusel Bars

Prep Time: 15 minutes   Bake Time: 40 minutes

1¾ cups all-purpose flour
1½ cups powdered sugar
½ cup unsweetened cocoa
1 cup (2 sticks) cold butter or margarine
1 (8-ounce) package cream cheese, softened
1 (14-ounce) can EAGLE® BRAND Sweetened Condensed Milk
   (NOT evaporated milk)
1 egg
2 teaspoons vanilla extract
½ cup chopped walnuts

1. Preheat oven to 350°F. In large bowl, combine flour, sugar and cocoa; cut in butter until crumbly (mixture will be dry). Reserve 2 cups crumb mixture. Press remaining crumb mixture firmly on bottom of ungreased 13×9-inch baking pan. Bake 15 minutes.

2. Meanwhile, in large bowl, beat cream cheese until fluffy. Gradually beat in **Eagle Brand** until smooth. Add egg and vanilla; mix well. Pour evenly over baked crust.

3. Combine reserved crumb mixture with walnuts; sprinkle evenly over cheese mixture. Bake 25 minutes or until bubbly. Cool. Chill. Cut into bars. Store covered in refrigerator.   *Makes 24 to 36 bars*

Pecan Pie Bars

Prep Time: 15 minutes   Bake Time: 40 minutes

2 cups all-purpose flour
½ cup powdered sugar
1 cup (2 sticks) cold butter or margarine
1 (14-ounce) can EAGLE® BRAND Sweetened Condensed Milk
   (NOT evaporated milk)
1 egg
1 teaspoon vanilla extract
1 (6-ounce) package almond brickle chips
1 cup chopped pecans

1. Preheat oven to 350°F (325°F for glass dish). In medium bowl, combine flour and sugar; cut in butter until crumbly. Press firmly on bottom of ungreased 13×9-inch baking pan. Bake 15 minutes.

2. Meanwhile, in medium bowl, beat **Eagle Brand,** egg and vanilla. Stir in chips and pecans. Spread evenly over baked crust.

3. Bake 25 minutes or until golden brown. Cool. Chill thoroughly. Cut into bars. Store covered in refrigerator. *Makes 36 bars*

Chocolate Almond Brownies

Prep Time: 15 minutes   **Bake Time:** 45 minutes

   1¼ **cups all-purpose flour, divided**
   2 **tablespoons sugar**
   ½ **cup (1 stick) cold butter or margarine**
   1 **cup chopped almonds, toasted and divided**
   1 **(14-ounce) can EAGLE® BRAND Sweetened Condensed Milk
      (NOT evaporated milk)**
   ¼ **cup unsweetened cocoa**
   1 **egg**
   2 **tablespoons amaretto liqueur *or* 1 teaspoon almond extract**
   ½ **teaspoon baking powder**
   6 **(1¼-ounce) white candy bars with almonds, broken into small
      pieces**

1. Preheat oven to 350°F. In medium bowl, combine 1 cup flour and sugar; cut in butter until crumbly. Add ¼ cup almonds. Press firmly on bottom of ungreased 9-inch round or square baking pan. Bake 15 minutes.

2. In large bowl, beat **Eagle Brand,** remaining ¼ cup flour, cocoa, egg, amaretto and baking powder until smooth. Stir in candy pieces and ½ cup almonds. Spread over baked crust.

3. Top with remaining ¼ cup almonds. Bake 30 minutes or until center is set. Cool. Cut into wedges. Store tightly covered at room temperature. *Makes 16 brownies*

Let's Celebrate

Celebrations mean having parties for holidays, family gatherings, birthdays and anniversaries, to name a few. With Eagle® Brand magic there's plenty of time to mingle because you can make party-perfect treats ahead of time, in no time. Simply make three or four of the fantastic desserts and treats in this chapter and then, at party time you'll be celebrating...Enjoy.

Top to bottom: Chewy Almond Squares (page 152) and Marbled Cheesecake Bars (page 153)

150

Chewy Almond Squares

Prep Time: 10 minutes   **Bake Time:** 30 to 37 minutes

1¼ cups graham cracker crumbs
¼ cup sugar
⅓ cup (⅔ stick) butter or margarine, melted
1 cup flaked coconut, toasted
1 cup chopped almonds, toasted*
1 (14-ounce) can EAGLE® BRAND Sweetened Condensed Milk
(NOT evaporated milk)

*1 cup chopped pecans or walnuts, toasted, may be substituted.

1. Preheat oven to 375°F. Line 9-inch square pan with foil. In medium bowl, combine crumbs, sugar and butter. Press into bottom of prepared pan. Bake 5 to 7 minutes.

2. Sprinkle crust with coconut and almonds; pour **Eagle Brand** evenly over surface.

3. Bake 25 to 30 minutes. Cool on wire rack. Cut into squares. Store covered at room temperature.   *Makes 16 squares*

Marbled Cheesecake Bars

Prep Time: 20 minutes   **Bake Time:** 45 to 50 minutes

2 cups finely crushed crème-filled chocolate sandwich cookies (about 24 cookies)
3 tablespoons butter or margarine, melted
3 (8-ounce) packages cream cheese, softened
1 (14-ounce) can EAGLE® BRAND Sweetened Condensed Milk (NOT evaporated milk)
3 eggs
2 teaspoons vanilla extract
2 (1-ounce) squares unsweetened chocolate, melted

1. Preheat oven to 300°F. Combine crumbs and butter; press firmly on bottom of ungreased 13×9-inch baking pan.

2. In large bowl, beat cream cheese until fluffy. Gradually beat in **Eagle Brand** until smooth. Add eggs and vanilla; mix well. Pour half the batter evenly over prepared crust.

3. Stir melted chocolate into remaining batter; spoon over vanilla batter. With table knife or metal spatula, gently swirl through batter to marble.

4. Bake 45 to 50 minutes or until set. Cool. Chill. Cut into bars. Store covered in refrigerator.   *Makes 24 to 36 bars*

 *Helpful Hint*

For best distribution of added ingredients (chocolate chips, nuts, etc.) or for even marbling, do not oversoften or overbeat the cream cheese.

153

Chocolate Nut Bars

Prep Time: 10 minutes   **Bake Time:** 33 to 38 minutes

1¾ **cups graham cracker crumbs**
½ **cup butter or margarine, melted**
1 **(14-ounce) can EAGLE® BRAND Sweetened Condensed Milk**
   (NOT evaporated milk)
2 **cups (12 ounces) semi-sweet chocolate chips, divided**
1 **teaspoon vanilla extract**
1 **cup chopped nuts**

1. Preheat oven to 375°F. Combine crumbs and butter; press firmly on bottom of 13×9-inch baking pan. Bake 8 minutes. Reduce oven temperature to 350°F.

2. In small saucepan, melt **Eagle Brand** with 1 cup chocolate chips and vanilla. Spread chocolate mixture over prepared crust. Top with remaining 1 cup chocolate chips then nuts; press down firmly.

3. Bake 25 to 30 minutes. Cool. Chill if desired. Cut into bars. Store loosely covered at room temperature.   *Makes 24 to 36 bars*

Chocolate Nut Bars

Party Mints

Prep Time: 30 minutes   **Stand Time:** 8 hours

   1 (14-ounce) can EAGLE® BRAND Sweetened Condensed Milk (NOT evaporated milk)
   1 (32-ounce) package powdered sugar
  ½ teaspoon peppermint extract
    Assorted colored granulated sugar or crystals

1. In medium bowl, beat **Eagle Brand** and half of powdered sugar until blended. Gradually add remaining powdered sugar and peppermint extract, beating until stiff.

2. Roll mixture into ½-inch balls; roll in desired sugar and place on lightly greased cooling rack. Let stand 8 hours. Store covered at room temperature. *Makes 2½ pounds*

 *Helpful Hint*

Eagle® Brand makes great cookies and bars, but don't forget that desserts made with Eagle® Brand contain condensed all-natural milk. This gives your family important bone-building calcium in every bite.

Streusel Caramel Bars

Prep Time: 25 minutes   **Bake Time:** 35 minutes

> 2 cups all-purpose flour
> ¾ cup packed brown sugar
> 1 egg, beaten
> ¾ cup (1½ sticks) cold butter or margarine, divided
> ¾ cup chopped nuts
> 24 caramels, unwrapped
> 1 (14-ounce) can EAGLE® BRAND Sweetened Condensed Milk
>   (NOT evaporated milk)

1. Preheat oven to 350°F. Grease 13×9-inch baking pan. In large bowl, combine flour, sugar and egg; cut in ½ cup butter until crumbly. Stir in nuts. Reserve 2 cups crumb mixture. Press remaining crumb mixture firmly on bottom of prepared pan. Bake 15 minutes.

2. Meanwhile, in heavy saucepan over low heat, melt caramels and remaining ¼ cup butter with **Eagle Brand.** Pour over baked crust.

3. Top with reserved crumb mixture. Bake 20 minutes or until bubbly. Cool. Cut into bars. Store loosely covered at room temperature.   *Makes 24 to 36 bars*

Toffee-Top Cheesecake Bars

Prep Time: 20 minutes   Bake Time: 40 minutes

1¼ cups all-purpose flour
1 cup powdered sugar
½ cup unsweetened cocoa powder
¼ teaspoon baking soda
¾ cup (1½ sticks) butter or margarine, softened
1 (8-ounce) package cream cheese, softened
1 (14-ounce) can EAGLE® BRAND Sweetened Condensed Milk
    (NOT evaporated milk)
2 eggs
1 teaspoon vanilla extract
1½ cups (8-ounce package) English toffee bits, divided

1. Preheat oven 350°F. Combine flour, powdered sugar, cocoa and baking soda in medium bowl; cut in butter until mixture is crumbly. Press into bottom of ungreased 13×9-inch baking pan. Bake 15 minutes.

2. Beat cream cheese until fluffy. Add **Eagle Brand,** eggs and vanilla; beat until smooth. Stir in 1 cup English toffee bits. Pour mixture over hot crust. Bake 25 minutes or until set and edges just begin to brown.

3. Remove from oven. Cool 15 minutes. Sprinkle remaining ½ cup English Toffee Bits evenly over top. Cool completely. Refrigerate several hours or until cold. Store leftovers covered in refrigerator.

Makes about 36 bars

Toffee-Top Cheesecake Bars

Fudgy Chocolate Pecan Bars

Prep Time: 20 minutes   **Bake Time:** 50 minutes

1 cup unsifted flour
⅔ cup sugar
½ cup unsweetened cocoa
½ teaspoon salt
¾ cup (1½ sticks) cold butter or margarine
2 eggs, divided
1 (14-ounce) can EAGLE® BRAND Sweetened Condensed Milk
  (NOT evaporated milk)
1½ teaspoons maple flavoring
1 cups pecan halves or pieces

1. Preheat oven to 350°F. In large bowl, combine flour, sugar, cocoa and salt; cut in cold butter until crumbly. Stir in 1 beaten egg. Press evenly into 13×9-inch baking pan.

2. Bake 25 minutes. Meanwhile, in medium bowl, beat in **Eagle Brand,** remaining 1 egg and flavoring; stir in pecan halves. Pour over baked crust, distributing pecan halves evenly.

3. Bake 25 minutes longer or until golden. Cut into bars. Store tightly covered at room temperature.   *Makes 24 to 36 bars*

Santa's Favorite Cookies

Sweet Treats for the Christmas Season

Brownies & Bars

Mystical Layered Bars

⅓ cup margarine or butter
1 cup graham cracker crumbs
½ cup old-fashioned or quick oats
1 can (14 ounces) sweetened condensed milk
1 cup flaked coconut
¾ cup semisweet chocolate chips
¾ cup raisins
1 cup coarsely chopped pecans

Preheat oven to 350°F. Melt margarine in 13×9-inch baking pan. Remove from oven. Sprinkle graham cracker crumbs and oats evenly over margarine; press down with fork. Drizzle condensed milk over oats. Layer coconut, chocolate chips, raisins and pecans over milk. Bake 25 to 30 minutes or until lightly browned. Cool in pan on wire rack 5 minutes. Cut into bars; cool completely.

Makes 3 dozen bars

Praline Brownies

Brownies

**1 package DUNCAN HINES®
  Chocolate Lovers Milk
  Chocolate Chunk Brownie Mix**
2 eggs
⅓ cup water
**⅓ cup vegetable oil plus additional
  for greasing**
¾ cup chopped pecans

Topping

¾ cup firmly packed brown sugar
¾ cup chopped pecans
¼ cup butter or margarine, melted
2 tablespoons milk
½ teaspoon vanilla extract

1. Preheat oven to 350°F. Grease 9-inch square pan.

2. For brownies, combine brownie mix, eggs, water, oil and ¾ cup pecans in large bowl. Stir with spoon until well blended, about 50 strokes. Spread in prepared pan. Bake at 350°F for 35 to 40 minutes. Remove from oven.

3. For topping, combine brown sugar, ¾ cup pecans, melted butter, milk and vanilla extract in medium bowl. Stir with spoon until well blended. Spread over hot brownies. Return to oven. Bake for 15 minutes longer or until topping is set. Cool completely in pan on wire rack. Cut into bars. *Makes about 16 brownies*

Chocolate Peanut Bars

½ cup butter or margarine, softened
¼ cup granulated sugar
1 cup packed brown sugar, divided
2 eggs, separated
1 teaspoon vanilla
2 cups all-purpose flour
2 teaspoons baking powder
½ teaspoon baking soda
¼ teaspoon salt
2 to 4 tablespoons milk
**1 cup (6 ounces) semisweet
  chocolate chips**
**¾ cup salted peanuts, coarsely
  chopped**

Preheat oven to 350°F. Lightly grease a 13×9-inch pan. Beat butter, granulated sugar and ¼ cup of brown sugar in large bowl. Beat in egg yolks and vanilla. Combine flour, baking powder, baking soda and salt in small bowl. Blend into butter mixture. Stir in enough milk to make a smooth, light dough. Press on bottom of prepared pan. Sprinkle chocolate chips over top; press lightly into dough. Beat egg whites in large bowl until stiff, but not dry. Gradually beat in remaining ¾ cup brown sugar. Spread mixture evenly over dough in pan; top with peanuts. Bake 25 to 30 minutes or until top is puffed, lightly browned and feels dry. Cut into 2×1-inch bars while still warm.
Makes about 5 dozen bars

Praline Brownies

Luscious Lemon Bars

2 cups all-purpose flour
1 cup butter
½ cup powdered sugar
4 teaspoons freshly grated lemon
   peel, divided
¼ teaspoon salt
1 cup granulated sugar
3 eggs
⅓ cup fresh lemon juice
   Powdered sugar

1. Preheat oven to 350°F. Grease 13×9-inch baking pan; set aside. Place flour, butter, powdered sugar, 1 teaspoon lemon peel and salt in food processor. Process until mixture forms coarse crumbs.

2. Press mixture evenly into prepared 13×9-inch baking pan. Bake 18 to 20 minutes or until golden brown.

3. Beat remaining 3 teaspoons lemon peel, granulated sugar, eggs and lemon juice in medium bowl with electric mixer at medium speed until well blended.

4. Pour mixture evenly over warm crust. Return to oven; bake 18 to 20 minutes or until center is set and edges are golden brown. Remove pan to wire rack; cool completely.

5. Dust with powdered sugar; cut into 2×1½-inch bars. Do not freeze.

Makes 3 dozen bars

Decadent Brownies

½ cup dark corn syrup
½ cup butter or margarine
6 squares (1 ounce *each*)
   semisweet chocolate
¾ cup sugar
3 eggs
1 cup all-purpose flour
1 cup chopped walnuts
1 teaspoon vanilla
   Fudge Glaze (recipe follows)

Preheat oven to 350°F. Grease 8-inch square pan. Combine corn syrup, butter and chocolate in large heavy saucepan. Place over low heat; stir until chocolate is melted and ingredients are blended. Remove from heat; blend in sugar. Stir in eggs, flour, chopped walnuts and vanilla. Spread batter evenly in prepared pan. Bake 20 to 25 minutes or just until center is set. *Do not overbake.* Meanwhile, prepare Fudge Glaze. Remove brownies from oven. Immediately spread glaze evenly over hot brownies. Cool in pan on wire rack. Cut into 2-inch squares.

Makes 16 brownies

Fudge Glaze

3 squares (1 ounce *each*)
   semisweet chocolate
2 tablespoons dark corn syrup
1 tablespoon butter or margarine
1 teaspoon light cream or milk

Combine chocolate, corn syrup and butter in small heavy saucepan. Stir over low heat until smooth; add cream.

Luscious Lemon Bars

Caramel Fudge Brownies

1 jar (12 ounces) hot caramel ice cream topping
1¼ cups all-purpose flour, divided
¼ teaspoon baking powder
Dash salt
4 squares (1 ounce *each*) unsweetened chocolate, coarsely chopped
¾ cup butter or margarine
2 cups sugar
3 eggs
2 teaspoons vanilla
¾ cup semisweet chocolate chips
¾ cup chopped pecans

Preheat oven to 350°F. Lightly grease 13×9-inch baking pan.

Combine caramel topping and ¼ cup flour in small bowl; set aside.

Combine remaining 1 cup flour, baking powder and salt in small bowl; mix well.

Place unsweetened chocolate squares and margarine in medium microwavable bowl. Microwave at HIGH 2 minutes or until margarine is melted; stir until chocolate is completely melted.

Stir sugar into melted chocolate with mixing spoon. Add eggs and vanilla; stir until combined.

Add flour mixture, stirring until well blended. Spread chocolate mixture evenly into prepared pan.

Bake 25 minutes. Immediately after removing brownies from oven, spread caramel mixture over brownies. Sprinkle top evenly with chocolate chips and pecans.

Return pan to oven; bake 20 to 25 minutes or until topping is golden brown and bubbling. *Do not overbake.* Cool brownies completely in pan on wire rack. Cut into 2×1½-inch bars.
Makes 3 dozen brownies

Almond Toffee Bars

¾ cup butter or margarine, softened
¾ cup packed brown sugar
1½ cups all-purpose flour
½ teaspoon almond extract
½ teaspoon vanilla extract
¼ teaspoon salt
1 package (6 ounces) semi-sweet real chocolate pieces
¾ cup BLUE DIAMOND® Chopped Natural Almonds, toasted

Preheat oven to 350°F. Cream butter and sugar; blend in flour. Add extracts and salt, mixing well. Spread in bottom of ungreased 13×9×2-inch baking pan. Bake in 350°F oven 15 to 20 minutes or until deep golden brown. Remove from oven and sprinkle with chocolate pieces. When chocolate has melted, spread evenly; sprinkle with almonds. Cut into bars; cool. *Makes about 40 bars*

Caramel Fudge Brownies

Yuletide Linzer Bars

1⅓ cups butter or margarine,
     softened
¾ cup sugar
1 egg
1 teaspoon grated lemon peel
2½ cups all-purpose flour
1½ cups whole almonds, ground
1 teaspoon ground cinnamon
¾ cup raspberry preserves
   Powdered sugar

Preheat oven to 350°F. Grease
13×9-inch baking pan.

Beat butter and sugar in large bowl with
electric mixer until creamy. Beat in egg
and lemon peel until blended. Mix in flour,
almonds and cinnamon until well blended.

Press 2 cups dough into bottom of
prepared pan. Spread preserves over
crust. Press remaining dough, a small
amount at a time, evenly over preserves.

Bake 35 to 40 minutes until golden
brown. Cool in pan on wire rack. Sprinkle
with powdered sugar; cut into bars.

Makes 36 bars

Black Russian Brownies

4 squares (1 ounce each)
     unsweetened chocolate
1 cup butter
¾ teaspoon ground black pepper
4 eggs, lightly beaten
1½ cups granulated sugar
1½ teaspoons vanilla
⅓ cup KAHLÚA® Liqueur
2 tablespoons vodka
1⅓ cups all-purpose flour
½ teaspoon salt
¼ teaspoon baking powder
1 cup chopped walnuts or toasted
     sliced almonds
   Powdered sugar (optional)

Preheat oven to 350°F. Line bottom of
13×9-inch baking pan with waxed paper.
Melt chocolate and butter with pepper in
small saucepan over low heat, stirring
until smooth. Remove from heat; cool.

Combine eggs, granulated sugar and
vanilla in large bowl; beat well. Stir in
cooled chocolate mixture, Kahlúa and
vodka. Combine flour, salt and baking
powder; add to chocolate mixture and
stir until blended. Add walnuts. Spread
evenly in prepared pan.

Bake just until wooden toothpick inserted
into center comes out clean, about
25 minutes. *Do not overbake.* Cool in pan
on wire rack. Cut into bars. Sprinkle with
powdered sugar.

Makes about 2½ dozen brownies

Yuletide Linzer Bars

Ooey Gooey Peanut Butter and Fudge Brownies

Batter

        WESSON® No-Stick Cooking
            Spray
    3 cups sugar
    1 cup (2 sticks) butter, softened
    ½ cup WESSON® Vegetable Oil
    1 tablespoon plus 1½ teaspoons
        vanilla
    6 eggs, at room temperature
    2¼ cups all-purpose flour
    1¼ cups cocoa
    1½ teaspoons baking powder
    ¾ teaspoon salt
    1 (10-ounce) bag peanut butter
        chips

Filling

    1½ cups PETER PAN® Creamy Peanut
        Butter
    ⅓ cup WESSON® Vegetable Oil
    ½ cup sugar
    3 tablespoons all-purpose flour
    3 eggs, at room temperature
    1 tablespoon vanilla

Frosting

    3 (1-ounce) bars unsweetened
        chocolate
    3 tablespoons PETER PAN® Creamy
        Peanut Butter
    2⅔ cups powdered sugar
    ¼ cup water
    1 teaspoon vanilla
    ¼ teaspoon salt

For batter, preheat oven to 350°F. Spray two 13×9×2-inch baking pans with Wesson® Cooking Spray. In a large bowl, beat sugar and butter until creamy. Add Wesson® Oil and vanilla. Add eggs, one at a time, beating well after each addition. In a small bowl, combine flour, cocoa, baking powder and salt; blend well. While beating, gradually add flour mixture to creamed mixture; mix well. Fold in peanut butter chips. Evenly spread ¼ of batter into one pan.

For filling, in a small bowl, cream together Peter Pan® Peanut Butter and Wesson® Oil. Add sugar and flour; blend well. Add eggs and vanilla; beat until smooth. Carefully spread ½ of filling mixture evenly over batter in pan. Top filling with an additional ¼ of batter and spread evenly. Gently cut through layers to create a marble effect throughout the brownies. Repeat process with remaining pan and remaining batter and remaining filling. Bake for 30 minutes. *Do not overbake.*

For frosting, meanwhile, in a medium saucepan, melt chocolate and peanut butter over LOW heat, stirring constantly. Remove from heat and stir in remaining ingredients; mix until smooth. If frosting is too thick, add an additional 1 to 3 tablespoons of water. Spread frosting over brownies immediately after baking. Cool in pans on wire racks.

Makes 3 dozen brownies

Ooey Gooey Peanut Butter
and Fudge Brownies

Crimson Ribbon Bars

6 tablespoons butter or margarine, softened
½ cup firmly packed brown sugar
1 teaspoon vanilla
½ cup all-purpose flour
¼ teaspoon baking soda
1½ cups old-fashioned oats
1 cup chopped walnuts
½ cup chopped BLUE RIBBON® Calimyrna or Mission Figs
⅓ cup SMUCKER'S® Red Raspberry Preserves

Heat oven to 375°F. Combine butter, brown sugar and vanilla; beat until well blended. Add flour and baking soda; mix well. Stir in oats and walnuts. Reserve ¾ cup mixture for topping. Press remaining oat mixture into 8-inch square baking pan. Combine figs and preserves; spread mixture to within ½ inch of edges. Sprinkle with reserved oat mixture; press lightly. Bake 25 to 30 minutes or until golden brown. Cool in pan; cut into bars.

Makes 20 bars

Oreo® Shazam Bars

28 OREO® Chocolate Sandwich Cookies
¼ cup margarine, melted
1 cup shredded coconut
1 cup white chocolate chips
½ cup chopped nuts
1 (14-ounce) can sweetened condensed milk

Finely roll 20 cookies. Mix cookie crumbs and margarine; spread over bottom of 9×9×2-inch baking pan, pressing lightly. Chop remaining cookies. Layer coconut, chips, nuts and chopped cookies in prepared pan; drizzle evenly with condensed milk. Bake at 350°F for 25 to 30 minutes or until golden and set. Cool completely. Cut into bars.

Makes 24 bars

Cocoa Brownies

1¼ cups all-purpose flour
1 cup packed light brown sugar
¾ cup sugar
½ cup egg substitute
½ cup margarine or butter, melted
¼ cup unsweetened cocoa
1½ teaspoons vanilla extract
⅓ cup PLANTERS® Pecans, chopped
Powdered sugar

1. Mix flour, sugars, egg substitute, melted margarine or butter and cocoa in large bowl until well blended. Stir in vanilla and pecans.

2. Spread in well greased 13×9×2-inch baking pan. Bake in preheated 350°F oven for 25 minutes or until done. Cool in pan on wire rack. Dust with powdered sugar; cut into bars. *Makes 3 dozen*

Preparation Time: 20 minutes

Cook Time: 25 minutes

Total Time: 45 minutes

Crimson Ribbon Bars

Triple Chocolate Brownies

    3 squares (1 ounce *each*)
        unsweetened chocolate,
        coarsely chopped
    2 squares (1 ounce *each*)
        semisweet chocolate, coarsely
        chopped
    ½ cup butter
    1 cup all-purpose flour
    ½ teaspoon salt
    ¼ teaspoon baking powder
    1½ cups sugar
    3 eggs
    1 teaspoon vanilla
    ¼ cup sour cream
    ½ cup milk chocolate chips
        Powdered sugar (optional)

Preheat oven to 350°F. Lightly grease
13×9-inch baking pan.

Place unsweetened chocolate, semisweet
chocolate and butter in medium
microwavable bowl. Microwave at HIGH
2 minutes or until butter is melted; stir until
chocolate is completely melted. Cool to
room temperature.

Combine flour, salt and baking powder in
small bowl.

Beat sugar, eggs and vanilla in large bowl
with electric mixer at medium speed until
slightly thickened. Beat in chocolate
mixture until well combined. Add flour
mixture; beat at low speed until blended.
Add sour cream; beat at low speed until
combined. Stir in chocolate chips. Spread
mixture evenly into prepared pan.

Bake 20 to 25 minutes or until toothpick
inserted into center comes out almost
clean. *Do not overbake.* Cool brownies

completely in pan on wire rack. Cut into
2-inch squares. Place powdered sugar in
fine-mesh strainer; sprinkle over brownies,
if desired.　　*Makes 2 dozen brownies*

Marshmallow Krispie Bars

    1 package DUNCAN HINES® Fudge
        Brownie Mix, Family Size
    1 package (10½ ounces) miniature
        marshmallows
    1½ cups semi-sweet chocolate chips
    1 cup creamy peanut butter
    1 tablespoon butter or margarine
    1½ cups crisp rice cereal

1. Preheat oven to 350°F. Grease bottom
of 13×9-inch pan.

2. Prepare and bake brownies following
package directions for basic recipe.
Remove from oven. Sprinkle
marshmallows on hot brownies. Return
to oven. Bake for 3 minutes longer.

3. Place chocolate chips, peanut butter
and butter in medium saucepan. Cook
over low heat, stirring constantly, until
chips are melted. Add rice cereal; mix
well. Spread mixture over marshmallow
layer. Refrigerate until chilled. Cut into
bars.　　*Makes about 2 dozen bars*

Tip: For a special presentation, cut
cookies into diamond shapes.

Triple Chocolate Brownies

Peanut Butter Chocolate Chippers

1 cup creamy peanut butter
1 cup packed light brown sugar
1 egg
¾ cup milk chocolate chips
Granulated sugar

Preheat oven to 350°F. Mix peanut butter, sugar and egg in bowl until blended. Add chips; mix well. Roll dough into 1½-inch balls; place 2 inches apart on ungreased cookie sheets. Dip fork into granulated sugar; press criss-cross onto each ball, flattening to ½-inch thickness. Bake 12 minutes or until set. Let cookies stand on cookie sheets 2 minutes. Remove cookies to wire racks; cool.   *Makes 24 cookies*

Note: This simple recipe is unusual because it doesn't contain any flour—but it still makes great cookies!

Chocolate Chips Thumbprint Cookies

1 cup HERSHEY'S Semi-Sweet Chocolate Chips, divided
½ cup sugar
¼ cup butter flavor shortening
¼ cup (½ stick) butter or margarine, softened
1 egg, separated
½ teaspoon vanilla extract
1 cup all-purpose flour
¼ teaspoon salt
1 cup finely chopped nuts

1. Heat oven to 350°F. Lightly grease cookie sheet. Place ¼ cup chocolate chips in small microwave-safe bowl. Microwave at HIGH (100%) 20 to 30 seconds or just until chocolate is melted and smooth when stirred; set aside to cool slightly.

2. Combine sugar, shortening, butter, reserved melted chocolate, egg yolk and vanilla; beat until well blended. Stir in flour and salt. Roll dough into 1-inch balls. With fork, slightly beat egg white. Dip each ball into egg white; roll in nuts to coat. Place about 1-inch apart on ungreased cookie sheet. Press center of each cookie with thumb to make indentation.

3. Bake 10 to 12 minutes or until set. Remove from oven; immediately place several chocolate chips in center of each cookie. Carefully remove from cookie sheet to wire rack. After several minutes, swirl melted chocolate in each thumbprint. Cool completely.

Makes about 2½ dozen cookies

Crispy Oat Drops

1 cup (2 sticks) butter or margarine, softened
½ cup granulated sugar
½ cup firmly packed light brown sugar
1 large egg
2 cups all-purpose flour
½ cup quick-cooking or old-fashioned oats, uncooked
1 teaspoon cream of tartar
½ teaspoon baking soda
¼ teaspoon salt
1¾ cups "M&M's"® Semi-Sweet Chocolate Mini Baking Bits
1 cup toasted rice cereal
½ cup shredded coconut
½ cup coarsely chopped pecans

Preheat oven to 350°F. In large bowl cream butter and sugars until light and fluffy; beat in egg. In medium bowl combine flour, oats, cream of tartar, baking soda and salt; blend flour mixture into creamed mixture. Stir in "M&M's"® Semi-Sweet Chocolate Mini Baking Bits, cereal, coconut and pecans. Drop by heaping tablespoonfuls about 2 inches apart onto ungreased cookie sheets. Bake 10 to 13 minutes or until lightly browned. Cool completely on wire racks. Store in tightly covered container.

Makes about 4 dozen cookies

Crispy Oat Drops

Mocha Crinkles

1⅓ cups firmly packed light brown
    sugar
½ cup vegetable oil
¼ cup low-fat sour cream
1 egg
1 teaspoon vanilla
1¾ cups all-purpose flour
¾ cup unsweetened cocoa powder
2 teaspoons instant espresso or
    coffee granules
1 teaspoon baking soda
¼ teaspoon salt
⅛ teaspoon ground black pepper
½ cup powdered sugar

1. Beat brown sugar and oil in medium bowl with electric mixer. Mix in sour cream, egg and vanilla. Set aside.

2. Mix flour, cocoa, espresso, baking soda, salt and pepper in another medium bowl.

3. Add flour mixture to brown sugar mixture; mix well. Refrigerate dough until firm, 3 to 4 hours.

4. Preheat oven to 350°F. Pour powdered sugar into shallow bowl. Set aside. Cut dough into 1-inch pieces; roll into balls. Roll balls in powdered sugar.

5. Bake on ungreased cookie sheets 10 to 12 minutes or until tops of cookies are firm to touch. *Do not overbake.* Cool on wire racks.   *Makes 6 dozen cookies*

Peanut Gems

2½ cups all-purpose flour
1 teaspoon baking powder
⅛ teaspoon salt
1 cup butter, softened
1 cup packed light brown sugar
2 eggs
2 teaspoons vanilla
1½ cups cocktail peanuts, finely
    chopped
Powdered sugar (optional)

Preheat oven to 350°F. Combine flour, baking powder and salt in small bowl.

Beat butter in large bowl with electric mixer at medium speed until smooth. Gradually beat in brown sugar; increase speed to medium-high and beat until light and fluffy. Beat in eggs, 1 at a time, until fluffy. Beat in vanilla. Gradually stir in flour mixture until blended. Stir in peanuts until blended.

Drop heaping tablespoonfuls of dough about 1 inch apart onto ungreased cookie sheets; flatten slightly with hands.

Bake 12 minutes or until set. Let cookies stand on cookie sheets 5 minutes; transfer to wire racks to cool completely. Dust cookies with powdered sugar, if desired. Store in airtight container.
            Makes about 2½ dozen cookies

Mocha Crinkles

Almond Milk Chocolate Chippers

½ cup slivered almonds
1¼ cups all-purpose flour
½ teaspoon baking soda
½ teaspoon salt
½ cup butter or margarine, softened
½ cup firmly packed light brown
    sugar
⅓ cup granulated sugar
1 egg
2 tablespoons almond-flavored
    liqueur
1 cup milk chocolate chips

1. Preheat oven to 350°F. To toast almonds, spread on baking sheet. Bake 8 to 10 minutes or until golden brown, stirring frequently. Remove almonds from pan and cool; set aside.

2. *Increase oven temperature to 375°F.* Place flour, baking soda and salt in small bowl; stir to combine.

3. Beat butter, brown sugar and granulated sugar in large bowl with electric mixer at medium speed until light and fluffy. Beat in egg until well blended. Beat in liqueur. Gradually add flour mixture. Beat at low speed until well blended. Stir in chips and almonds with spoon.

4. Drop rounded teaspoonfuls of dough 2 inches apart onto ungreased cookie sheets.

5. Bake 9 to 10 minutes or until edges are golden brown. Let cookies stand on cookie sheets 2 minutes. Remove cookies with spatula to wire racks; cool completely.
    Makes about 3 dozen cookies

Frosty's Colorful Cookies

1¼ cups firmly packed light brown
    sugar
¾ Butter Flavor* CRISCO® Stick or
    ¾ cup Butter Flavor CRISCO
    all-vegetable shortening
2 tablespoons milk
1 tablespoon vanilla
1 egg
1¾ cups all-purpose flour
1 teaspoon salt
¾ teaspoon baking soda
2 cups red and green candy-coated
    chocolate pieces

*Butter Flavor Crisco is artificially flavored.

1. Heat oven to 375°F. Place sheets of foil on countertop for cooling cookies.

2. Place brown sugar, ¾ cup shortening, milk and vanilla in large bowl. Beat at medium speed of electric mixer until well blended. Add egg; beat well.

3. Combine flour, salt and baking soda. Add to shortening mixture; beat at low speed just until blended. Stir in candy-coated chocolate pieces.

4. Drop dough by rounded measuring tablespoonfuls 3 inches apart onto ungreased baking sheets.

5. Bake one baking sheet at a time at 375°F for 8 to 10 minutes for chewy cookies, or 11 to 13 minutes for crisp cookies. *Do not overbake.* Cool 2 minutes on baking sheet. Remove cookies to foil to cool completely.
    Makes about 3 dozen cookies

Almond Milk Chocolate Chippers

Hershey's Great American Chocolate Chip Cookies

   1 cup (2 sticks) butter, softened
   ¾ cup granulated sugar
   ¾ cup packed light brown sugar
   1 teaspoon vanilla extract
   2 eggs
   2¼ cups all-purpose flour
   1 teaspoon baking soda
   ½ teaspoon salt
   2 cups (12-ounce package)
      HERSHEY'S Semi-Sweet
      Chocolate Chips
   1 cup chopped nuts (optional)

1. Heat oven to 375°F.

2. Beat butter, granulated sugar, brown sugar and vanilla in large bowl until creamy. Add eggs; beat well. Stir together flour, baking soda and salt; gradually add to butter mixture, beating well. Stir in chocolate chips and nuts, if desired. Drop dough by rounded teaspoonfuls onto ungreased cookie sheet.

3. Bake 8 to 10 minutes or until lightly browned. Cool slightly; remove from cookie sheet to wire rack. Cool completely.
Makes about 6 dozen cookies

Skor® & Chocolate Chip Cookies: Omit 1 cup HERSHEY'S Semi-Sweet Chocolate Chips and nuts; replace with 1 cup finely chopped SKOR® bars. Drop onto cookie sheets and bake as directed.

Great American Ice Cream Sandwiches: Prepare cookies as directed. Place one small scoop slightly softened vanilla ice cream between flat sides of two cookies. Gently press together. Wrap and freeze.

Spicy Oatmeal Raisin Cookies

   1 package DUNCAN HINES® Moist
      Deluxe Spice Cake Mix
   4 egg whites
   1 cup quick-cooking oats (not
      instant or old-fashioned),
      uncooked
   ½ cup vegetable oil
   ½ cup raisins

1. Preheat oven to 350°F. Grease cookie sheets.

2. Combine cake mix, egg whites, oats and oil in large mixer bowl. Beat on low speed with electric mixer until blended. Stir in raisins. Drop by rounded teaspoons onto prepared cookie sheets.

3. Bake 7 to 9 minutes or until lightly browned. Cool 1 minute on cookie sheets. Remove to cooling racks; cool completely.
Makes about 4 dozen cookies

Ultimate Chippers

2½ cups all-purpose flour
1 teaspoon baking soda
½ teaspoon salt
1 cup butter or margarine, softened
1 cup packed light brown sugar
½ cup granulated sugar
2 eggs
1 tablespoon vanilla
1 cup semisweet chocolate chips
1 cup milk chocolate chips
1 cup vanilla milk chips
½ cup coarsely chopped pecans
   (optional)

Preheat oven to 375°F. Combine flour, baking soda and salt in medium bowl.

Beat butter, brown sugar and granulated sugar in large bowl until light and fluffy. Beat in eggs and vanilla. Add flour mixture to butter mixture; beat until well blended. Stir in chips and pecans, if desired.

Drop by heaping teaspoonfuls 2 inches apart onto ungreased cookie sheets. Bake 10 to 12 minutes or until edges are golden brown. Let cookies stand on cookie sheets 2 minutes. Remove cookies to wire racks; cool completely.
Makes about 6 dozen cookies

Molasses Spice Cookies

1 cup granulated sugar
¾ cup shortening
¼ cup molasses
1 egg, beaten
2 cups all-purpose flour
2 teaspoons baking soda
1 teaspoon ground cinnamon
1 teaspoon ground cloves
1 teaspoon ground ginger
¼ teaspoon dry mustard
¼ teaspoon salt
½ cup granulated brown sugar

1. Preheat oven to 375°F. Grease cookie sheets; set aside.

2. Beat granulated sugar and shortening about 5 minutes in large bowl until light and fluffy. Add molasses and egg; beat until fluffy.

3. Combine flour, baking soda, cinnamon, cloves, ginger, mustard and salt in medium bowl. Add to shortening mixture; mix until just combined.

4. Place brown sugar in shallow dish. Roll tablespoonfuls of dough into 1-inch balls; roll in sugar to coat. Place 2 inches apart on prepared cookie sheets. Bake 15 minutes or until lightly browned. Let cookies stand on cookie sheets 2 minutes. Remove cookies to wire racks; cool completely.
Makes about 6 dozen cookies

Two-Toned Spritz Cookies

1 square (1 ounce) unsweetened
    chocolate, coarsely chopped
1 cup (2 sticks) butter or margarine,
    softened
1 cup sugar
1 egg
1 teaspoon vanilla
2¼ cups all-purpose flour
¼ teaspoon salt

Melt chocolate in small heavy saucepan over low heat, stirring constantly; set aside. Beat butter and sugar in large bowl until light and fluffy. Beat in egg and vanilla. Combine flour and salt in medium bowl; gradually add to butter mixture. Reserve 2 cups dough. Beat chocolate into dough in bowl until smooth. Cover both doughs and refrigerate until firm enough to handle, about 20 minutes.

Preheat oven to 400°F. Roll out vanilla dough between two sheets of waxed paper to ½-inch thickness. Cut into 5×4-inch rectangles. Place chocolate dough on sheet of waxed paper. Using waxed paper to hold dough, roll back and forth to form a log about 1 inch in diameter. Cut into 5-inch-long logs. Place chocolate log in center of vanilla rectangle. Wrap vanilla dough around log and fit into cookie press fitted with star disc. Press dough onto ungreased cookie sheets 1½ inches apart. Bake about 10 minutes or until just set. Remove cookies with spatula to wire racks; cool completely.

Makes about 4 dozen cookies

Double Nut Chocolate Chip Cookies

1 package DUNCAN HINES® Moist
    Deluxe® Yellow Cake Mix
½ cup butter or margarine, melted
1 egg
1 cup semisweet chocolate chips
½ cup finely chopped pecans
1 cup sliced almonds, divided

1. Preheat oven to 375°F. Grease cookie sheets.

2. Combine cake mix, butter and egg in large bowl. Mix at low speed with electric mixer until just blended. Stir in chocolate chips, pecans and ¼ cup almonds. Shape rounded tablespoonfuls of dough into balls. Place remaining ¾ cup almonds in shallow bowl. Press tops of cookies in almonds. Place 1 inch apart on prepared cookie sheets.

3. Bake 9 to 11 minutes or until lightly browned. Cool 2 minutes on cookie sheets. Remove to cooling racks.

Makes 3 to 3½ dozen cookies

Two-Toned Spritz Cookies

Maple Walnut Meringues

⅓ cup powdered sugar
½ cup plus ⅓ cup ground walnuts, divided
¾ cup packed light brown sugar
3 egg whites, at room temperature
Pinch salt
⅛ teaspoon cream of tartar
1 teaspoon maple extract

Place 1 oven rack in the top third of oven and 1 oven rack in the bottom third of oven. Preheat oven to 300°F. Line 2 large cookie sheets with foil, shiny side up. Stir powdered sugar and ½ cup walnuts with fork in medium bowl; set aside. Crumble brown sugar into small bowl; set aside. Beat egg whites and salt in large bowl with electric mixer at high speed until foamy. Add cream of tartar; beat 30 seconds or until mixture forms soft peaks. Sprinkle brown sugar 1 tablespoon at a time over egg white mixture; beat at high speed until each addition is completely absorbed. Beat 2 to 3 minutes or until mixture forms stiff peaks. Beat in maple extract at low speed. Fold in walnut mixture with large rubber spatula. Drop level tablespoonfuls of dough to form mounds about 1 inch apart on prepared cookie sheets. Sprinkle cookies with remaining ⅓ cup ground walnuts. Bake 25 minutes or until cookies feel dry on surface but remain soft inside. (Rotate cookie sheets from top to bottom halfway through baking time.) Slide foil with cookies onto wire racks; cool completely. Carefully remove cookies from foil. Store in airtight container with wax paper between layers of cookies. Cookies are best the day they are baked.

Makes about 3 dozen cookies

Chocolate Drop Sugar Cookies

⅔ cup butter or margarine, softened
1 cup sugar
1 egg
1½ teaspoons vanilla extract
1½ cups all-purpose flour
½ cup HERSHEY'S Cocoa
½ teaspoon baking soda
¼ teaspoon salt
⅓ cup buttermilk or sour milk*
Additional sugar

*To sour milk: Use 1 teaspoon white vinegar plus milk to equal ⅓ cup.

1. Heat oven to 350°F. Lightly grease cookie sheet.

2. Beat butter and sugar in large bowl until well blended. Add egg and vanilla; beat until light and fluffy. Stir together flour, cocoa, baking soda and salt; add alternately with buttermilk to butter mixture. Using ice cream scoop or ¼ cup measuring cup, drop dough about 2 inches apart onto prepared cookie sheet.

3. Bake 13 to 15 minutes or until cookie springs back when touched lightly in center. While cookies are on cookie sheet, sprinkle lightly with additional sugar. Cool slightly; remove from cookie sheet to wire rack. Cool completely.

Makes about 1 dozen cookies

Maple Walnut Meringues

Oatmeal Raisin Cookies

¾ **cup all-purpose flour**
¾ **teaspoon salt**
½ **teaspoon baking soda**
½ **teaspoon ground cinnamon**
¾ **cup butter or margarine, softened**
¾ **cup granulated sugar**
¾ **cup packed light brown sugar**
1 **egg**
1 **tablespoon water**
3 **teaspoons vanilla, divided**
3 **cups uncooked quick-cooking or old-fashioned oats**
1 **cup raisins**
½ **cup powdered sugar**
1 **tablespoon milk**

Preheat oven to 375°F. Grease cookie sheets; set aside. Combine flour, salt, baking soda and cinnamon in small bowl.

Beat butter, granulated sugar and brown sugar in large bowl with electric mixer at medium speed until light and fluffy. Add egg, water and 2 teaspoons vanilla; beat well. Add flour mixture; beat at low speed just until blended. Stir in oats with spoon. Stir in raisins.

Drop tablespoonfuls of dough 2 inches apart onto prepared cookie sheets.

Bake 10 to 11 minutes or until edges are golden brown. Let cookies stand 2 minutes on cookie sheets; transfer to wire racks to cool completely.

For glaze, stir powdered sugar, milk and remaining 1 teaspoon vanilla in small bowl until smooth. Drizzle over cookies with fork or spoon.
Makes about 4 dozen cookies

Cocoa Nut Bundles

1 **can (8 ounces) refrigerated quick crescent dinner rolls**
2 **tablespoons butter or margarine, softened**
1 **tablespoon granulated sugar**
2 **teaspoons HERSHEY®S Cocoa**
¼ **cup chopped nuts**
Powdered sugar

1. Heat oven to 375°F. Unroll dough and separate to form 8 triangles on ungreased cookie sheet.

2. Combine butter, granulated sugar and cocoa in small bowl. Add nuts; mix thoroughly. Divide chocolate mixture evenly among triangles, placing on wide end of triangle. Take dough on either side of mixture and pull up and over mixture, tucking ends under. Continue rolling dough toward opposite point.

3. Bake 9 to 10 minutes or until golden brown. Sprinkle with powdered sugar; serve warm. *Makes 8 rolls*

Oatmeal Raisin Cookies

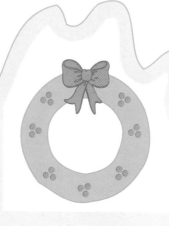

Chocolate Bonanza

Festive Fudge Blossoms

1 box (18.25 ounces) chocolate fudge cake mix
¼ cup butter or margarine, softened
1 egg, slightly beaten
¾ to 1 cup finely chopped walnuts
48 chocolate star candies

Preheat oven to 350°F. Cut butter into cake mix in large bowl until coarse crumbs form. Stir in egg and 2 tablespoons water until well blended. Shape dough into ½-inch balls; roll in walnuts, pressing nuts gently into dough. Place about 2 inches apart onto ungreased baking sheets. Bake cookies 12 minutes or until puffed and nearly set. Place chocolate star in center of each cookie; bake 1 minute. Cool 2 minutes on baking sheet. Remove cookies from baking sheets to wire rack to cool completely.

Makes 4 dozen cookies

Czech Bear Paws

4 cups toasted ground hazelnuts
2 cups all-purpose flour
1 tablespoon unsweetened cocoa
powder
1 teaspoon ground cinnamon
½ teaspoon ground nutmeg
¼ teaspoon salt
1 cup butter plus 3 teaspoons
butter, softened, divided
1 cup powdered sugar
1 egg yolk
½ cup melted chocolate chips
Slivered almonds, halved

1. Preheat oven to 350°F. Place hazelnuts, flour, cocoa, cinnamon, nutmeg and salt in medium bowl; stir to combine.

2. Beat 1 cup butter, powdered sugar and egg yolk in large bowl with electric mixer at medium speed until light and fluffy. Gradually add flour mixture. Beat at low speed until soft dough forms.

3. Grease 3 madeleine pans with remaining softened butter, 1 teaspoon per pan; dust with flour. (If only 1 madeleine pan is available, thoroughly wash, dry, regrease and flour after baking each batch. Cover remaining dough with plastic wrap; let stand at room temperature.) Press level tablespoonfuls of dough into each mold.

4. Bake 12 minutes or until lightly browned. Let cookies stand in pan 3 minutes. Carefully loosen cookies from pan with point of small knife. Invert pan over wire racks; tap lightly to release cookies. Let stand 2 minutes. Turn cookies shell-side up; cool completely.

5. Pipe squiggle of melted chocolate on curved end of each cookie; place slivered almond halves in melted chocolate for claws. Let stand at room temperature 1 hour or until set. Store tightly covered at room temperature.

Makes about 5 dozen cookies

Note: These cookies do not freeze well.

Triple Chocolate Cookies

1 package DUNCAN HINES® Moist
Deluxe® Swiss Chocolate Cake
Mix
½ cup butter or margarine, melted
1 egg
½ cup semi-sweet chocolate chips
½ cup milk chocolate chips
½ cup coarsely chopped white
chocolate
½ cup chopped pecans

1. Preheat oven to 375°F.

2. Combine cake mix, melted butter and egg in large bowl. Beat at low speed with electric mixer until blended. Stir in all 3 chocolates and pecans.

3. Drop by rounded tablespoonfuls onto ungreased baking sheets. Bake at 375°F 9 to 11 minutes. Cool 1 minute on baking sheet. Remove to cooling racks.

Makes 3½ to 4 dozen cookies

Tip: Cookies may be stored in an airtight container in freezer for up to 6 months.

Czech Bear Paws

Chocolate Peanut Butter Cup Cookies

Cookies

1 cup semi-sweet chocolate chips
2 squares (1 ounce each)
    unsweetened baking chocolate
1 cup sugar
½ Butter Flavor* CRISCO® Stick or
    ½ cup Butter Flavor CRISCO®
    all-vegetable shortening
2 eggs
1 teaspoon salt
1 teaspoon vanilla
1½ cups plus 2 tablespoons
    all-purpose flour
½ teaspoon baking soda
¾ cup finely chopped peanuts
36 miniature peanut butter cups,
    unwrapped

Drizzle

1 cup peanut butter chips

*Butter Flavor Crisco is artificially flavored.

1. Heat oven to 350°F. Place sheets of foil on countertop for cooling cookies.

2. For cookies, combine chocolate chips and chocolate squares in microwave-safe measuring cup or bowl. Microwave at 50% (MEDIUM). Stir after 2 minutes. Repeat until smooth (or melt on rangetop in small saucepan on very low heat). Cool slightly.

3. Combine sugar and ½ cup shortening in large bowl. Beat at medium speed of electric mixer until blended and crumbly. Beat in eggs, one at a time, then salt and vanilla. Reduce speed to low. Add chocolate slowly. Mix until well blended. Stir in flour and baking soda with spoon until well blended. Shape dough into 1¼-inch balls. Roll in nuts. Place 2 inches apart on ungreased baking sheet.

4. Bake at 350°F for 8 to 10 minutes or until set. *Do not overbake.* Press peanut butter cup into center of each cookie immediately. Press cookie against cup. Cool 2 minutes on baking sheet before removing to cooling rack. Cool completely.

5. For drizzle, place peanut butter chips in heavy resealable sandwich bag. Seal. Microwave at 50% (MEDIUM). Knead bag after 1 minute. Repeat until smooth (or melt by placing bag in hot water). Cut tiny tip off corner of bag. Squeeze out and drizzle over cookies.

Makes 3 dozen cookies

Helpful Hint

Chocolate should be stored in a cool, dry place (60°F to 70°F) to avoid the appearance of "bloom," a gray-white film on the surface.

S'More Snack Treats

44 squares HONEY MAID® Honey Grahams (2 sleeves)
3 tablespoons margarine
1 (10-ounce) package marshmallows
¾ cup miniature semisweet chocolate chips

1. Break grahams into bite-size pieces; set aside.

2. Heat margarine in large saucepan over medium heat until melted. Add marshmallows, stirring constantly until melted.

3. Stir broken crackers into marshmallow mixture to coat evenly. Spread mixture into lightly greased 13×9×2-inch pan; sprinkle with chocolate chips, pressing lightly with greased hands.

4. Chill at least 20 minutes before cutting into squares. *Makes 12 s'mores*

Preparation Time: 15 minutes

Cook Time: 20 minutes

Chill Time: 20 minutes

Total Time: 55 minutes

Festive Chocolate Chip Cookies

1 package DUNCAN HINES® Moist Deluxe® White Cake Mix
¼ cup firmly packed light brown sugar
1 egg
¾ cup vegetable oil
1 package (6 ounces) semi-sweet chocolate chips
½ cup chopped pecans or walnuts
Assorted decors

1. Preheat oven to 350°F.

2. Combine cake mix, brown sugar, egg and oil in large bowl. Beat at low speed with electric mixer until blended. Stir in chocolate chips and pecans. Form dough into 1½-inch ball. Dip top of ball in decors. Place ball decor-side up on ungreased baking sheets. Repeat with remaining dough placing balls 2 inches apart on baking sheets. Bake at 350°F 10 to 12 minutes or until light golden brown around edges. Cool 2 minutes on baking sheets. Remove to cooling racks. Cool completely. Store in airtight container. *Makes 3 to 3½ dozen cookies*

Tip: Cool baking sheet completely before baking each batch of cookies.

S'More Snack Treats

Marshmallow Sandwich Cookies

⅔ cup butter
1¼ cups sugar
¼ cup light corn syrup
1 egg
1 teaspoon vanilla
2 cups all-purpose flour
½ cup unsweetened cocoa powder
2 teaspoons baking soda
¼ teaspoon salt
Sugar for rolling
24 large marshmallows

Preheat oven to 350°F. Beat butter and 1¼ cups sugar in large bowl until light and fluffy. Beat in corn syrup, egg and vanilla. Combine flour, cocoa, baking soda and salt in medium bowl; add to butter mixture. Beat until well blended. Cover and refrigerate dough 15 minutes or until firm enough to roll into balls.

Place sugar in shallow dish. Roll tablespoonfuls of dough into 1-inch balls; roll in sugar to coat. Place cookies 3 inches apart on ungreased cookie sheets. Bake 10 to 12 minutes or until set. Remove cookies to wire rack; cool completely.

To assemble sandwiches, place one marshmallow on flat side of one cookie on paper plate. Microwave at HIGH 12 seconds or until marshmallow just begins to melt. Immediately place another cookie, flat side down, on top of hot marshmallow; press together slightly.

*Makes about 2 dozen
sandwich cookies*

Santa's Chocolate Cookies

1 cup margarine or butter
⅔ cup semisweet chocolate chips
¾ cup sugar
1 egg
½ teaspoon vanilla
2 cups all-purpose flour
Apricot jam, melted semisweet chocolate, chopped almonds, frosting, coconut or colored sprinkles

Preheat oven to 350°F. Melt margarine and chocolate together in small saucepan over low heat or microwave 2 minutes at HIGH until completely melted. Combine chocolate mixture and sugar in large bowl. Add egg and vanilla; stir well. Add flour; stir well. Refrigerate 30 minutes or until firm.

Shape dough into 1-inch balls. Place 1 inch apart on ungreased cookie sheets. If desired, flatten balls with bottom of drinking glass, shape into logs or make a depression in center and fill with apricot jam.

Bake 8 to 10 minutes or until set. Remove to wire racks to cool completely. Decorate as desired with melted chocolate, almonds, frosting, coconut and colored sprinkles.

Makes about 3 dozen cookies

Marshmallow Sandwich Cookies

Nutty Clusters

2 squares (1 ounce *each*)
    unsweetened chocolate
½ cup butter or margarine, softened
1 cup granulated sugar
1 egg
⅓ cup buttermilk
1 teaspoon vanilla
1¾ cups all-purpose flour
½ teaspoon baking soda
1 cup mixed salted nuts, chopped
    Easy Chocolate Icing
    (recipe follows)

Preheat oven to 400°F. Line cookie sheets with parchment paper or leave ungreased. Melt chocolate in top of double boiler over hot, not boiling, water. Remove from heat; cool. Beat butter and granulated sugar in large bowl until smooth. Beat in egg, melted chocolate, buttermilk and vanilla until light. Stir in flour, baking soda and nuts. Drop dough by teaspoonfuls 2 inches apart onto cookie sheets. Bake 8 to 10 minutes or until almost no imprint remains when touched. Immediately remove cookies from cookie sheets to wire racks. While cookies bake, prepare Easy Chocolate Icing. Frost cookies while still warm.

Makes about 4 dozen cookies

Easy Chocolate Icing

2 squares (1 ounce *each*)
    unsweetened chocolate
2 tablespoons butter or margarine
2 cups powdered sugar
2 to 3 tablespoons water

Melt chocolate and butter in small heavy saucepan over low heat, stirring until completely melted. Add powdered sugar and water, mixing until smooth.

Chocolate Macaroons

1 can (8 ounces) almond paste
½ cup powdered sugar
2 egg whites
12 ounces semisweet baking
    chocolate or chips, melted
2 tablespoons all-purpose flour
    Powdered sugar (optional)

Preheat oven to 300°F. Line cookie sheets with parchment paper; set aside.

Beat almond paste, sugar and egg whites in large bowl with electric mixer at medium speed 1 minute. Beat in chocolate until well combined. Beat in flour at low speed.

Spoon dough into pastry bag fitted with rosette tip. Pipe 1½-inch spirals 1 inch apart onto prepared cookie sheets. Pipe all cookies at once; dough will get stiff upon standing.

Bake 20 minutes or until set. Carefully remove parchment paper to countertop; cool completely.

Peel cookies off parchment paper. Sprinkle powdered sugar over cookies, if desired.

Makes about 3 dozen cookies

Nutty Clusters

Holiday Favorites

....

Candy Cane Cookies

....

  1 cup sugar
  ⅔ cup margarine or butter, softened
  ½ cup egg substitute
  2 teaspoons vanilla extract
  1 teaspoon almond extract
  3 cups all-purpose flour
  1 teaspoon DAVIS® Baking Powder
  ½ teaspoon red food coloring

1. Beat sugar and margarine or butter in large bowl with mixer at medium speed until creamy. Beat in egg substitute, vanilla and almond extracts. Mix flour and baking powder; stir into margarine mixture.

continued on page 208

Candy Cane Cookies, continued

2. Divide dough in half; tint half with red food coloring. Wrap each half and refrigerate at least 2 hours.

3. Divide each half into 32 pieces. Roll each piece into a 5-inch rope. Twist 1 red and 1 white rope together and bend 1 end to form candy cane shape. Place on ungreased baking sheets.

4. Bake in preheated 350°F oven for 8 to 10 minutes or just until set and lightly golden. Remove from sheets; cool on wire racks. Store in airtight container.

Makes 32 cookies

Helpful Hint

Looking for something different to take to all your holiday gatherings? Decorate a metal tin with rubber stamps for a crafty look, and fill it with candy cane cookies and an assortment of flavored coffees. It's perfect for a "homey" hostess gift.

Cocoa Kiss Cookies

1 cup (2 sticks) butter or margarine, softened
⅔ cup sugar
1 teaspoon vanilla extract
1⅔ cups all-purpose flour
¼ cup HERSHEY'S Cocoa
1 cup finely chopped pecans
1 bag (9 ounces) HERSHEY'S KISSES® Milk Chocolates
Powdered sugar

1. Beat butter, sugar and vanilla in large bowl until creamy. Stir together flour and cocoa; gradually add to butter mixture, beating until blended. Add pecans; beat until well blended. Refrigerate dough about 1 hour or until firm enough to handle.

2. Heat oven to 375°F. Remove wrappers from chocolate pieces. Mold scant tablespoon of dough around each chocolate piece, covering completely. Shape into balls. Place on ungreased cookie sheet.

3. Bake 10 to 12 minutes or until set. Cool slightly, about 1 minute; remove from cookie sheet to wire rack. Cool completely. Roll in powdered sugar. Roll in sugar again just before serving, if desired.

Makes about 4½ dozen cookies

Top to bottom: Cocoa Kiss Cookies and Hershey's Great American Chocolate Chip Cookies (page 186)

Slice 'n' Bake Ginger Wafers

½ cup butter or margarine, softened
1 cup packed brown sugar
¼ cup light molasses
1 egg
2 teaspoons ground ginger
1 teaspoon grated orange peel
¼ teaspoon salt
¼ teaspoon ground cinnamon
¼ teaspoon ground cloves
2 cups all-purpose flour

1. Beat butter, sugar and molasses in large bowl until light and fluffy. Add egg, ginger, orange peel, salt, cinnamon and cloves; beat until well blended. Stir in flour until well blended. (Dough will be very stiff.)

2. Divide dough in half. Roll each half into 8×1½-inch log. Wrap logs in waxed paper or plastic wrap; refrigerate at least 5 hours or up to 3 days.

3. Preheat oven to 350°F. Cut dough into ¼-inch-thick slices. Place about 2 inches apart on ungreased baking sheets. Bake 12 to 14 minutes or until set. Remove from baking sheet to wire rack to cool.
Makes about 4½ dozen cookies

Serving Suggestion: Dip half of each cookie in melted white chocolate or drizzle cookies with a glaze of 1¼ cups powdered sugar and 2 tablespoons orange juice. Or, cut cookie dough into ⅛-inch-thick slices; bake and sandwich melted caramel candy or peanut butter between cookies.

Snowball Cookies

1 cup margarine or butter, softened
1 cup sugar
1 teaspoon vanilla extract
2 cups all-purpose flour
1½ cups PLANTERS® Pecans, finely ground
¼ teaspoon salt
½ cup powdered sugar

1. Beat margarine, sugar and vanilla in large bowl with mixer at medium speed until creamy. Blend in flour, pecans and salt. Refrigerate 1 hour.

2. Shape dough into 1-inch balls. Place on ungreased baking sheets, 2 inches apart. Bake in preheated 350°F oven for 10 to 12 minutes. Remove from sheets; cool on wire racks. Dust with powdered sugar. Store in airtight container.
Makes 6 dozen cookies

Preparation Time: 15 minutes

Chill Time: 1 hour

Cook Time: 10 minutes

Total Time: 1 hour and 25 minutes

Rum Fruitcake Cookies

1 cup sugar
¾ cup vegetable shortening
3 eggs
⅓ cup orange juice
1 tablespoon rum extract
3 cups all-purpose flour
2 teaspoons baking powder
1 teaspoon baking soda
1 teaspoon salt
2 cups (8 ounces) candied fruit
1 cup raisins
1 cup nuts, coarsely chopped

1. Preheat oven to 375°F. Lightly grease cookie sheets; set aside. Beat sugar and shortening in large bowl until fluffy. Add eggs, orange juice and rum extract; beat 2 minutes longer.

2. Combine flour, baking powder, baking soda and salt in small bowl. Add fruit, raisins and nuts. Stir into creamed mixture. Drop dough by rounded teaspoonfuls 2 inches apart onto prepared cookie sheets. Bake 10 to 12 minutes or until golden. Let cookies stand on cookie sheets 2 minutes. Remove to wire rack; cool completely.

Makes about 6 dozen cookies

Holiday Wreath Cookies

1 package (20 ounces) refrigerated sugar cookie dough
2 cups shredded coconut
2 to 3 drops green food color
1 container (16 ounces) ready-to-spread French vanilla frosting
Green sugar or small cinnamon candies

1. Preheat oven to 350°F. Divide cookie dough in half (keep half of dough refrigerated until needed). Roll dough out on well-floured surface to ⅛-inch-thick rectangle. Cut with cookie cutters to resemble wreaths. Repeat with remaining half of dough.

2. Place cookies about 2 inches apart on ungreased baking sheets. Bake 7 to 9 minutes or until edges are lightly browned. Remove cookies from baking sheets to wire rack to cool completely.

3. Place coconut in resealable plastic food storage bag. Add food color; seal bag and shake until coconut is evenly colored. Frost cookies with frosting and decorate with coconut or green sugar and cinnamon candies.

Makes about 2 dozen cookies

Prep and Bake Time: 30 minutes

Rum Fruitcake Cookies

Fruitcake Slices

1 cup butter or margarine, softened
1 cup powdered sugar
1 egg
1 teaspoon vanilla extract
1½ cups coarsely chopped candied
    fruit (fruitcake mix)
½ cup coarsely chopped walnuts
2½ cups all-purpose unsifted flour,
    divided
¾ to 1 cup flaked coconut

Beat butter in large bowl with electric mixer at medium speed until smooth. Add powdered sugar; beat until well blended. Add egg and vanilla; beat until well blended.

Combine candied fruit and walnuts in medium bowl. Stir ¼ cup flour into fruit mixture. Add remaining 2¼ cups flour to butter mixture; beat at low speed until blended. Stir in fruit mixture with spoon.

Shape dough into 2 logs, each about 2 inches in diameter and 5½ inches long. Spread coconut evenly on sheet of waxed paper. Roll logs in coconut, coating evenly. Wrap each log in plastic wrap. Refrigerate 2 to 3 hours or overnight, or freeze up to 1 month. (Let frozen logs stand at room temperature about 10 minutes before slicing and baking.)

Preheat oven to 350°F. Grease cookie sheets. Cut logs into ¼-inch-thick slices; place 1 inch apart on cookie sheets.

Bake 13 to 15 minutes or until edges are golden brown. Transfer to wire racks to cool.　　*Makes about 4 dozen cookies*

Honey Ginger Snaps

2 cups all-purpose flour
1 tablespoon ground ginger
2 teaspoons baking soda
⅛ teaspoon salt
⅛ teaspoon ground cloves
½ cup vegetable shortening
¼ cup butter, softened
1½ cups sugar, divided
¼ cup honey
1 egg
1 teaspoon vanilla

Preheat oven to 350°F. Grease cookie sheets. Combine flour, ginger, baking soda, salt and cloves in medium bowl.

Beat shortening and butter in large bowl with electric mixer at medium speed until smooth. Gradually beat in 1 cup sugar until blended; increase speed to high and beat until light and fluffy. Beat in honey, egg and vanilla until fluffy. Gradually stir in flour mixture until blended.

Shape mixture into 1-inch balls. Place remaining ½ cup sugar in shallow bowl; roll balls in sugar to coat. Place 2 inches apart on prepared cookie sheets.

Bake 10 minutes or until golden brown. Let cookies stand on cookie sheets 5 minutes; transfer to wire racks to cool completely.　　*Makes 42 cookies*

Fruitcake Slices

Oatmeal Almond Balls

⅓ **cup honey**
2 **egg whites**
½ **teaspoon ground cinnamon**
⅛ **teaspoon salt**
1½ **cups uncooked quick oats**
¼ **cup sliced almonds, toasted**

1. Preheat oven to 350°F. Combine honey, egg whites, cinnamon and salt in large bowl; mix well. Add oats and toasted almonds; mix well.

2. Drop by rounded teaspoonfuls onto ungreased nonstick cooking sheet. Bake 12 minutes or until lightly browned. Remove to wire rack to cool.

Makes 24 servings

Thumbprint Cookies

1 **cup butter or margarine**
¼ **cup sugar**
1 **teaspoon almond extract**
2 **cups all-purpose flour**
½ **teaspoon salt**
1 **cup finely chopped nuts, if desired**
  SMUCKER'S® Preserves or Jams (any flavor)

Combine butter and sugar; beat until light and fluffy. Blend in almond extract. Add flour and salt; mix well.

Shape level tablespoonfuls of dough into balls; roll in nuts. Place on ungreased cookie sheets; flatten slightly. Indent centers; fill with preserves or jams.

Bake at 400°F for 10 to 12 minutes or just until lightly browned.

Makes 2½ dozen cookies

Snow-Covered Almond Crescents

1 **cup (2 sticks) margarine or butter, softened**
¾ **cup powdered sugar**
½ **teaspoon almond extract *or***
  2 **teaspoons vanilla extract**
2 **cups all-purpose flour**
¼ **teaspoon salt (optional)**
1 **cup QUAKER® Oats (quick or old-fashioned, uncooked)**
½ **cup finely chopped almonds**
  Additional powdered sugar

Preheat oven to 325°F. Beat margarine, ¾ cup powdered sugar and almond extract until fluffy. Add flour and salt; mix until well blended. Stir in oats and almonds. Shape level measuring tablespoonfuls of dough into crescents. Place on ungreased cookie sheet about 2 inches apart.

Bake 14 to 17 minutes or until bottoms are light golden brown. Remove to wire rack. Sift additional powdered sugar generously over warm cookies. Cool completely. Store tightly covered.

Makes about 4 dozen cookies

Oatmeal Almond Balls

Jolly Peanut Butter Gingerbread Cookies

1⅔ cups (10-ounce package) REESE'S® Peanut
    Butter Chips
¾ cup (1½ sticks) butter or margarine,
    softened
1 cup packed light brown sugar
1 cup dark corn syrup
2 eggs
5 cups all-purpose flour
1 teaspoon baking soda
½ teaspoon ground cinnamon
¼ teaspoon ground ginger
¼ teaspoon salt

continued on page 220

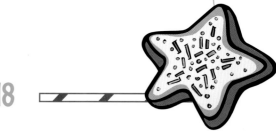

Jolly Peanut Butter Gingerbread Cookies, continued

1. Place peanut butter chips in small microwave-safe bowl. Microwave at HIGH (100%) 1 to 2 minutes or until chips are melted when stirred. Beat melted peanut butter chips and butter in large bowl until well blended. Add brown sugar, corn syrup and eggs; beat until light and fluffy. Stir together flour, baking soda, cinnamon, ginger and salt. Add half of flour mixture to butter mixture; beat on low speed of electric mixer until smooth. Stir in remaining flour mixture with wooden spoon until well blended. Divide into thirds; wrap each in plastic wrap. Refrigerate at least 1 hour or until dough is firm enough to roll.

2. Heat oven to 325°F.

3. Roll 1 dough portion at a time to ⅛-inch thickness on lightly floured surface. Cut into holiday shapes with floured cookie cutters. Place on ungreased cookie sheet.

4. Bake 10 to 12 minutes or until set and lightly browned. Cool slightly; remove from cookie sheet to wire rack. Cool completely. Frost and decorate as desired.
Makes about 6 dozen cookies

Holiday Bits Cutout Cookies

1 cup (2 sticks) butter or margarine, softened
1 cup sugar
2 eggs
2 teaspoons vanilla extract
2½ cups all-purpose flour
½ teaspoon baking powder
½ teaspoon salt
HERSHEY'S Holiday Candy Coated Bits

1. Beat butter, sugar, eggs and vanilla in large bowl on low speed of electric mixer just until blended. Stir together flour, baking powder and salt; add to butter mixture, stirring until well blended.

2. Divide dough in half. Cover; refrigerate 1 to 2 hours or until firm enough to handle. Heat oven to 400°F. On lightly floured surface, roll each half of the dough to about ¼-inch thickness.

3. Cut into tree, wreath, star or other shapes with 2½-inch cookie cutters. Place on ungreased cookie sheet. Press candy coated bits into cutouts.

4. Bake 6 to 8 minutes or until edges are firm and bottoms are very lightly browned. Remove from cookie sheet to wire rack. Cool completely.
Makes about 3½ dozen cookies

Holiday Bits Cutout Cookies

Christmas Cookie Pops

**1 package (20 ounces) refrigerated
sugar cookie dough
All-purpose flour (optional)
20 to 24 (4-inch) lollipop sticks
Royal Icing (recipe follows)
6 ounces almond bark (vanilla or
chocolate), or butterscotch
chips
Vegetable shortening
Assorted small candies**

1. Preheat oven to 350°F. Grease cookie sheets; set aside.

2. Remove dough from wrapper according to package directions.

3. Sprinkle dough with flour to minimize sticking, if necessary. Cut dough in half. Reserve 1 half; refrigerate remaining dough.

4. Roll reserved dough to ⅓-inch thickness. Cut out cookies using 3¼- or 3½-inch Christmas cookie cutters. Place lollipop sticks on cookies so that tips of sticks are imbedded in cookies. Carefully turn cookies with spatula so sticks are in back; place on prepared cookie sheets. Repeat with remaining dough.

5. Bake 7 to 11 minutes or until edges are lightly browned. Cool cookies on sheets 2 minutes. Remove cookies to wire racks; cool completely.

6. Prepare Royal Icing.

7. Melt almond bark in medium microwavable bowl according to package directions. Add 1 or more tablespoons shortening if coating is too thick. Hold cookies over bowl; spoon coating over cookies. Scrape excess coating from cookie edges. Decorate with Royal Icing and small candies immediately. Place cookies on wire racks set over waxed paper; let dry.

Makes 20 to 24 cookies

Royal Icing

**2 to 3 egg whites
2 to 4 cups powdered sugar
1 tablespoon lemon juice
Liquid food coloring (optional)**

*Use only grade A clean, uncracked eggs.

Beat 2 egg whites in medium bowl with electric mixer until peaks just begin to hold their shape. Add 2 cups sugar and lemon juice; beat for 1 minute. If consistency is too thin for piping, gradually add more sugar until desired result is achieved; if it is too thick, add another egg white. Divide icing among several small bowls and tint to desired colors. Keep bowls tightly covered until ready to use.

Christmas Cookie Pops

Holiday Chocolate Shortbread Cookies

1 cup (2 sticks) butter, softened
1¼ cups powdered sugar
1 teaspoon vanilla extract
½ cup HERSHEY®S Dutch Processed Cocoa or HERSHEY®S Cocoa
1¾ cups all-purpose flour
1⅔ cups (10-ounce package) HERSHEY®S Premier White Chips

1. Heat oven to 300°F. Beat butter, powdered sugar and vanilla in large bowl until creamy. Add cocoa; beat until well blended. Gradually add flour; stir well.

2. Roll or pat dough to ¼-inch thickness on lightly floured surface or between 2 pieces of wax paper. Cut into holiday shapes using star, tree, wreath or other cookie cutters. Reroll dough scraps, cutting cookies until dough is used. Place on ungreased cookie sheet.

3. Bake 15 to 20 minutes or just until firm. Immediately place white chips, flat side down, in decorative design on warm cookies. Cool slightly; remove from cookie sheet to wire rack. Cool completely.

Makes about 4½ dozen (2-inch diameter) cookies

Note: For more even baking, place similar shapes and sizes of cookies on same cookie sheet.

Prep Time: 30 minutes

Bake Time: 15 minutes

Cool Time: 30 minutes

Chocolate Reindeer

1 cup butter or margarine, softened
1 cup sugar
1 egg
1 teaspoon vanilla
2 ounces semisweet chocolate, melted
2¼ cups all-purpose flour
1 teaspoon baking powder
¼ teaspoon salt
Royal Icing (recipe follows)
Assorted small candies

1. Beat butter and sugar in large bowl at high speed of electric mixer until fluffy. Beat in egg and vanilla. Add melted chocolate; mix well. Add flour, baking powder and salt; mix well. Cover and refrigerate about 2 hours or until firm.

2. Preheat oven to 325°F. Grease 2 cookie sheets; set aside.

3. Divide dough in half. Reserve 1 half; wrap remaining dough in plastic wrap and refrigerate.

4. Roll reserved dough on well-floured surface to ¼-inch thickness. Cut with reindeer cookie cutter. Place 2 inches apart on prepared cookie sheet. Chill 10 minutes.

5. Bake 13 to 15 minutes or until set. Cool completely on cookie sheets. Repeat steps with remaining dough.

6. Prepare Royal Icing. To decorate, pipe assorted colored icing on reindeer and add small candies.

Makes 16 (4-inch) reindeer

Royal Icing

2 to 3 egg whites
2 to 4 cups powdered sugar
1 tablespoon lemon juice
   Liquid food coloring (optional)

*Use only grade A clean, uncracked eggs.

Beat 2 egg whites in medium bowl with electric mixer until peaks just begin to hold their shape. Add 2 cups sugar and lemon juice; beat 1 minute. If consistency is too thin for piping, gradually add more sugar until desired result is achieved; if it is too thick, add another egg white. Divide icing among several small bowls and tint to desired colors. Keep bowls tightly covered until ready to use.

Note: For best results, let cookies dry overnight, uncovered, before storing in airtight container at room temperature.

Gingerbread Cookies

¾ cup light or dark molasses
¾ cup margarine or butter
¾ cup packed light brown sugar
4½ cups all-purpose flour
   1 tablespoon ground ginger
   2 teaspoons ground cinnamon
   1 teaspoon DAVIS® Baking Powder
   ½ teaspoon baking soda
   ½ teaspoon ground nutmeg
¼ cup egg substitute
   Decorator icing, raisins and
      assorted candies, optional

1. Heat molasses, margarine or butter and brown sugar in small saucepan over medium heat to a boil, stirring occasionally. Remove from heat; cool.

2. Mix flour, ginger, cinnamon, baking powder, baking soda and nutmeg in large bowl. Blend egg substitute into molasses mixture. Stir molasses mixture into flour mixture until smooth. Wrap dough; refrigerate 1 hour.

3. Divide dough in half. Roll dough to ¼-inch thickness on floured surface. Cut with floured 5×3-inch gingerbread man cutter. Place onto lightly greased baking sheets.

4. Bake in preheated 350°F oven for 10 to 12 minutes or until lightly browned. Remove from sheets; cool on wire racks. Decorate as desired with icing, raisins and candies.   *Makes 2 dozen cookies*

Preparation Time: 30 minutes

Chill Time: 1 hour

Cook Time: 10 minutes

Total Time: 1 hour and 40 minutes

Christmas Tree Platter

**Christmas Ornament Cookie
Dough (recipe follows)
2 cups sifted powdered sugar
2 tablespoons milk or lemon juice
Assorted food colors, colored
    sugars and assorted small
    decors**

1. Prepare Christmas Ornament Cookie Dough. Divide dough in half. Reserve 1 half; refrigerate remaining dough. Roll reserved half of dough to ⅛-inch thickness.

2. Preheat oven to 350°F. Cut out tree shapes with cookie cutters. Place on ungreased cookie sheets.

3. Bake 10 to 12 minutes or until edges are lightly browned. Remove to wire racks; cool completely.

4. Repeat with remaining half of dough. Reroll scraps; cut into small circles for ornaments, squares and rectangles for gift boxes and tree trunks.

5. Bake 8 to 12 minutes, depending on size of cookies.

6. Mix powdered sugar and milk for icing. Tint most of icing green and a smaller amount red or other colors for ornaments and boxes. Spread green icing on trees. Sprinkle ornaments and boxes with colored sugars or decorate as desired.

7. Arrange cookies on flat platter to resemble tree as shown in photo.

Makes about 1 dozen cookies

Christmas Ornament Cookie Dough

**2¼ cups all-purpose flour
 ¼ teaspoon salt
 1 cup granulated sugar
 ¾ cup butter or margarine, softened
 1 egg
 1 teaspoon vanilla
 1 teaspoon almond extract**

Combine flour and salt in medium bowl. Beat sugar and butter in large bowl at medium speed of electric mixer until fluffy. Beat in egg, vanilla and almond extract. Gradually add flour mixture. Beat at low speed until well blended. Form dough into 2 discs; wrap in plastic wrap and refrigerate 30 minutes or until firm.

Helpful Hint

Use this beautiful Christmas Tree Platter cookie as your centerpiece for this year's holiday family dinner. It is sure to receive lots of "oohs" and "ahs!"

Stained Glass Cookies

½ cup margarine or butter, softened
½ cup sugar
½ cup honey
¼ cup egg substitute
1 teaspoon vanilla extract
3 cups all-purpose flour
1 teaspoon DAVIS® Baking Powder
½ teaspoon baking soda
½ teaspoon salt
5 (.90-ounce) rolls Five Flavor or Fancy Fruits LIFE SAVERS® Candy

1. Beat together margarine or butter, sugar, honey, egg substitute and vanilla in bowl with mixer until creamy. Mix in flour, baking powder, baking soda and salt. Cover; refrigerate at least 2 hours.

2. Roll dough on a lightly floured surface to ¼-inch thickness. Cut dough into desired shapes with 2½- to 3-inch floured cookie cutters. Trace a smaller version of cookie shape on dough leaving a ½- to ¾-inch border of dough. Cut out and remove dough from center of cookies; set aside. Place cut-out shapes on baking sheets lined with foil. Repeat with reserved dough, re-rolling scraps as necessary.

3. Crush each color of candy separately between two layers of wax paper. Spoon crushed candy inside centers of cut-out cookie shapes.

4. Bake in preheated 350°F oven for 6 to 8 minutes or until candy is melted and cookies are lightly browned. Cool cookies completely before removing from foil.

Makes 3½ dozen

Preparation Time: 1 hour
Chill Time: 2 hours
Cook Time: 6 minutes
Total Time: 3 hours and 6 minutes

Butter Cookies

¾ cup butter or margarine, softened
¼ cup granulated sugar
¼ cup packed light brown sugar
1 egg yolk
1¾ cups all-purpose flour
¾ teaspoon baking powder
⅛ teaspoon salt

1. Combine butter, sugars and egg yolk in medium bowl. Add flour, baking powder and salt; mix well. Cover; refrigerate until firm, about 4 hours or overnight.

2. Preheat oven to 350°F.

3. Roll dough on lightly floured surface to ¼-inch thickness; cut into desired shapes with cookie cutters. Place on ungreased cookie sheets.

4. Bake 8 to 10 minutes or until edges begin to brown. Remove to wire racks; cool completely.

Makes about 2 dozen cookies

Stained Glass Cookies

Molded Scotch Shortbread

1½ cups all-purpose flour
¼ teaspoon salt
¾ cup butter, softened
⅓ cup sugar
1 egg

Preheat oven to temperature recommended by shortbread mold manufacturer. Combine flour and salt in medium bowl. Beat butter and sugar in large bowl with electric mixer at medium speed until light and fluffy. Beat in egg. Gradually add flour mixture; beat at low speed. Spray 10-inch ceramic shortbread mold with nonstick cooking spray. Press dough firmly into mold. Bake, cool and remove from mold according to manufacturer's directions.

Makes 1 shortbread mold

Almond Crescents

1 cup butter, softened
⅓ cup granulated sugar
1¾ cups all-purpose flour
¼ cup cornstarch
1 teaspoon vanilla
1½ cups ground toasted almonds*
Chocolate Glaze (recipe follows)
and powdered sugar

*To toast almonds, spread on cookie sheet. Bake at 325°F for 4 minutes or until fragrant and golden.

Preheat oven to 325°F. Beat butter and granulated sugar in large bowl until creamy. Mix in flour, cornstarch and vanilla. Stir in almonds. Shape tablespoonfuls of dough into crescents. Place 2 inches apart on ungreased cookie sheets. Bake 22 to 25 minutes or until light brown. Cool 1 minute. Remove to wire racks; cool completely. Prepare Chocolate Glaze; drizzle over cookies. Allow chocolate to set. Before serving, sprinkle with powdered sugar.
Makes about 3 dozen cookies

Chocolate Glaze: Place ½ cup semisweet chocolate chips and 1 tablespoon butter or margarine in small resealable plastic food storage bag. Place bag in bowl of hot water for 2 to 3 minutes or until chocolate is softened. Dry with paper towel. Knead until chocolate mixture is smooth. Cut off very tiny corner of bag. Drizzle chocolate mixture over cookies.

Chocolate Covered Cherry Cookies

1 cup sugar
½ cup butter, softened
1 egg
1½ teaspoons vanilla
1½ cups all-purpose flour
¼ cup unsweetened cocoa powder
¼ teaspoon baking powder
¼ teaspoon baking soda
¼ teaspoon salt
42 maraschino cherries, drained
reserving 4 to 5 teaspoons juice
1 (6-ounce) package semisweet
chocolate pieces
½ cup sweetened condensed milk

Beat sugar and butter in large bowl until light and fluffy. Blend in egg and vanilla. Combine flour, cocoa, baking powder, baking soda and salt in small bowl. Add to sugar mixture; mix well. Shape dough into 1-inch balls; place on ungreased cookie sheet. Indent centers; fill each with 1 cherry. Combine chocolate pieces and sweetened condensed milk in small saucepan; stir over low heat until smooth. Blend in enough cherry juice to reach spreading consistency. Drop 1 teaspoon chocolate mixture over each cherry, spreading to cover cherry. Bake in preheated 350°F oven 12 minutes or until set. *Makes 3½ dozen cookies*

Favorite recipe from ***Wisconsin Milk Marketing Board***

Almond Crescents

Danish Cookie Rings

½ cup blanched almonds
2 cups all-purpose flour
¾ cup sugar
¼ teaspoon baking powder
1 cup butter, cut into small pieces
1 egg
1 tablespoon milk
1 tablespoon vanilla
15 candied red cherries
15 candied green cherries

Grease cookie sheets; set aside. Process almonds in food processor until ground, but not pasty. Place almonds, flour, sugar and baking powder in large bowl. Cut butter into flour mixture with pastry blender or 2 knives until mixture is crumbly.

Beat egg, milk and vanilla in small bowl with fork until well blended. Add egg mixture to flour mixture; stir until soft dough forms.

Spoon dough into pastry bag fitted with medium star tip. Pipe 3-inch rings 2 inches apart onto prepared cookie sheets. Refrigerate rings 15 minutes or until firm.

Preheat oven to 375°F. Cut cherries into quarters. Cut green cherries into halves; cut each half into 4 slivers. Press red cherry quarter onto each ring where ends meet. Arrange 2 green cherry slivers on either side of red cherry to form leaves. Bake 8 to 10 minutes or until golden. Remove cookies to wire racks; cool completely.

Makes about 5 dozen cookies

Mocha Biscotti

2½ cups all-purpose flour
½ cup unsweetened cocoa
2 teaspoons DAVIS® Baking Powder
1¼ cups sugar
¾ cup egg substitute
¼ cup margarine or butter, melted
4 teaspoons instant coffee powder
½ teaspoon vanilla extract
⅓ cup PLANTERS® Slivered Almonds, chopped
Powdered sugar (optional)

1. Mix flour, cocoa and baking powder in small bowl; set aside.

2. Beat sugar, egg substitute, melted margarine, coffee powder and vanilla in large bowl with mixer at medium speed for 2 minutes. Stir in flour mixture and almonds.

3. Divide dough in half. Shape each portion of dough with floured hands into 14×2-inch log on greased baking sheet. (Dough will be sticky.) Bake in preheated 350°F oven for 25 minutes.

4. Remove from oven and cut each log on a diagonal into 16 (1-inch) slices. Place biscotti, cut-side up, on baking sheets; return to oven and bake 10 to 15 minutes more on each side or until lightly toasted.

5. Remove from sheets. Cool completely on wire racks. Dust biscotti tops with powdered sugar if desired. Store in airtight container.   *Makes 32 biscotti*

Preparation Time: 20 minutes
Cook Time: 35 minutes
Total Time: 55 minutes

Danish Cookie Rings

Linzer Sandwich Cookies

1⅓ cups all-purpose flour
¼ teaspoon baking powder
¼ teaspoon salt
¾ cup granulated sugar
½ cup butter, softened
1 egg
1 teaspoon vanilla
Powdered sugar (optional)
Seedless raspberry jam

Combine flour, baking powder and salt in small bowl. Beat granulated sugar and butter in medium bowl with electric mixer at medium speed until light and fluffy. Beat in egg and vanilla. Gradually add flour mixture. Beat at low speed until dough forms. Divide dough in half; cover and refrigerate 2 hours or until firm.

Preheat oven to 375°F. Working with 1 portion at a time, roll out dough on lightly floured surface to ³⁄₁₆-inch thickness. Cut dough into desired shapes with floured cookie cutters. Cut out equal numbers of each shape. (If dough becomes too soft, refrigerate several minutes before continuing.) Cut 1-inch centers out of half the cookies of each shape. Reroll trimmings and cut out more cookies. Place cookies 1½ to 2 inches apart on ungreased cookie sheets. Bake 7 to 9 minutes or until edges are lightly brown. Let cookies stand on cookie sheets 1 to 2 minutes. Remove cookies to wire racks; cool completely.

Sprinkle cookies with holes with powdered sugar, if desired. Spread 1 teaspoon jam on flat side of whole cookies, spreading almost to edges. Place cookies with holes, flat side down, over jam to create sandwich.

Makes about 2 dozen cookies

Chunky Butter Christmas Cookies

1¼ cups butter, softened
1 cup packed brown sugar
½ cup dairy sour cream
1 egg
2 teaspoons vanilla
1½ cups all-purpose flour
1 teaspoon baking soda
1 teaspoon salt
1½ cups old fashioned or quick oats, uncooked
1 (10-ounce) package white chocolate pieces
1 cup flaked coconut
1 (3½-ounce) jar macadamia nuts, coarsely chopped

Beat butter and sugar in large bowl until light and fluffy. Blend in sour cream, egg and vanilla. Add combined flour, baking soda and salt; mix well. Stir in oats, white chocolate pieces, coconut and nuts. Drop rounded teaspoonfuls of dough, 2 inches apart, onto ungreased cookie sheet. Bake in preheated 375°F oven 10 to 12 minutes or until edges are lightly browned. Cool 1 minute; remove to cooling rack.

Makes 5 dozen cookies

Favorite recipe from **Wisconsin Milk Marketing Board**

Linzer Sandwich Cookies

Mincemeat Pastries

3½ cups all-purpose flour
¾ cup granulated sugar
½ teaspoon salt
½ cup (1 stick) butter, chilled
8 tablespoons vegetable shortening
1 cup buttermilk
1 cup mincemeat
¼ cup powdered sugar (optional)

1. Combine flour, granulated sugar and salt in large bowl; set aside.

2. Cut butter into 1-inch chunks. Add butter and shortening to flour mixture. Cut in with pastry blender or 2 knives until mixture resembles coarse crumbs. Drizzle buttermilk over top; toss just until mixture comes together into a ball.

3. Turn out dough onto lightly floured work surface; fold in half and flatten to about ½ inch thick. Knead about eight times. Divide dough in half; press each half into ½-inch-thick disk. Wrap in plastic wrap and refrigerate at least 30 minutes.

4. Let dough rest at room temperature 10 minutes. Preheat oven to 350°F. Lightly grease cookie sheets; set aside. Roll one disk of dough into 18×12-inch rectangle on lightly floured work surface. Cut into 24 (3-inch) squares. Place heaping ½ teaspoon mincemeat in center of each square. Fold one corner about ⅔ of the way over the filling; fold opposite corner ⅔ of the way over the filling.

5. Place 2 inches apart on prepared cookie sheets. Repeat with remaining dough.

6. Bake 20 minutes or until lightly browned. Remove cookies to wire rack; cool completely. Sprinkle tops of pastries lightly with powdered sugar, if desired.
Makes 4 dozen cookies

Banana Crescents

½ cup chopped almonds, toasted
6 tablespoons sugar, divided
½ cup margarine, cut into pieces
1½ cups plus 2 tablespoons all-purpose flour
⅛ teaspoon salt
1 extra-ripe, medium DOLE® Banana, peeled
2 to 3 ounces semisweet chocolate chips

• Pulverize almonds with 2 tablespoons sugar.

• Beat margarine, almonds, remaining 4 tablespoons sugar, flour and salt.

• Purée banana; add to almond mixture and mix until well blended.

• Roll tablespoonfuls of dough into logs, then shape into crescents. Place on ungreased cookie sheet. Bake in 375°F oven 25 minutes or until golden. Cool on wire rack.

• Melt chocolate in microwavable dish at MEDIUM (50% power) 1½ to 2 minutes, stirring once. Dip ends of cookies in chocolate. Refrigerate until chocolate is set.
Makes 2 dozen cookies

Date Pinwheel Cookies

1¼ cups dates, pitted and finely
    chopped
¾ cup orange juice
½ cup granulated sugar
1 tablespoon butter
3 cups plus 1 tablespoon
    all-purpose flour, divided
2 teaspoons vanilla, divided
4 ounces cream cheese
¼ cup vegetable shortening
1 cup packed brown sugar
2 eggs
1 teaspoon baking soda
½ teaspoon salt

1. Heat dates, orange juice, granulated sugar, butter and 1 tablespoon flour in medium saucepan over medium heat. Cook, stirring frequently, 10 minutes or until thick; remove from heat. Stir in 1 teaspoon vanilla; set aside to cool.

2. Beat cream cheese, shortening and brown sugar about 3 minutes in large bowl until light and fluffy. Add eggs and remaining 1 teaspoon vanilla; beat 2 minutes longer.

3. Combine 3 cups flour, baking soda and salt in medium bowl. Add to shortening mixture; stir just until blended. Divide dough in half. Roll one half of dough on lightly floured work surface into 12×9-inch rectangle. Spread half of date mixture over dough. Spread evenly, leaving ¼-inch border on top short edge. Starting at short side, tightly roll up dough jelly-roll style. Wrap in plastic wrap; freeze for at least 1 hour. Repeat with remaining dough.

4. Preheat oven to 350°F. Grease cookie sheets. Unwrap dough. Using heavy thread or dental floss, cut dough into ¼-inch slices. Place slices 1 inch apart on prepared cookie sheets.

5. Bake 12 minutes or until lightly browned. Let cookies stand on cookie sheets 2 minutes. Remove cookies to wire rack; cool completely.
Makes 6 dozen cookies

Make Ahead Tip

Wrap rolls of dough in plastic wrap and twist the ends tightly to seal. Place the wrapped rolls in tall plastic drinking glasses before freezing so rolls will not flatten from resting on freezer shelf.

My Favorite Recipes

Favorite recipe: _____

Favorite recipe from: _____

Ingredients: _____

_____

_____

_____

_____

_____

Method: _____

_____

_____

_____

_____

_____

_____

_____

_____

_____

Favorite recipe: _____

Favorite recipe from: _____

Ingredients: _____

_____

_____

_____

_____

_____

Method: _____

_____

_____

_____

_____

_____

_____

_____

_____

_____

_____

_____

Favorite recipe: _____

Favorite recipe from: _____

Ingredients: _____

_____

_____

_____

_____

_____

Method: _____

_____

_____

_____

_____

_____

_____

_____

_____

_____

Favorite recipe: _____

Favorite recipe from: _____

Ingredients: _____

_____

_____

_____

_____

_____

Method: _____

_____

_____

_____

_____

_____

_____

_____

_____

_____

My Favorite Recipes

Favorite recipe: _____

Favorite recipe from: _____

Ingredients: _____

_____

_____

_____

_____

_____

Method: _____

_____

_____

_____

_____

_____

_____

_____

_____

_____

My Favorite Recipes

Favorite recipe: _____

Favorite recipe from: _____

Ingredients: _____

_____

_____

_____

_____

_____

Method: _____

_____

_____

_____

_____

_____

_____

_____

_____

_____

_____

My Favorite Recipes

Favorite recipe: _____

Favorite recipe from: _____

Ingredients: _____

_____

_____

_____

_____

_____

Method: _____

_____

_____

_____

_____

_____

_____

_____

_____

_____

Favorite recipe: _____

Favorite recipe from: _____

Ingredients: _____

_____

_____

_____

_____

_____

Method: _____

_____

_____

_____

_____

_____

_____

_____

_____

_____

_____

My Favorite Recipes

Favorite recipe: _____

Favorite recipe from: _____

Ingredients: _____

_____

_____

_____

_____

_____

Method: _____

_____

_____

_____

_____

_____

_____

_____

_____

_____

Favorite recipe: _____

Favorite recipe from: _____

Ingredients: _____

_____

_____

_____

_____

_____

Method: _____

_____

_____

_____

_____

_____

_____

_____

_____

_____

_____

_____

My Favorite Recipes

Favorite recipe: _____

Favorite recipe from: _____

Ingredients: _____

_____

_____

_____

_____

_____

Method: _____

_____

_____

_____

_____

_____

_____

_____

_____

_____

_____

Favorite recipe: _____

Favorite recipe from: _____

Ingredients: _____

_____

_____

_____

_____

_____

Method: _____

_____

_____

_____

_____

_____

_____

_____

_____

_____

_____

Favorite recipe: _____

Favorite recipe from: _____

Ingredients: _____

_____

_____

_____

_____

_____

Method: _____

_____

_____

_____

_____

_____

_____

_____

_____

_____

My Favorite Recipes

Favorite recipe: _____

Favorite recipe from: _____

Ingredients: _____

_____

_____

_____

_____

_____

Method: _____

_____

_____

_____

_____

_____

_____

_____

_____

_____

_____

Favorite recipe: _____

Favorite recipe from: _____

Ingredients: _____

_____

_____

_____

_____

_____

Method: _____

_____

_____

_____

_____

_____

_____

_____

_____

_____

Favorite recipe: _____

Favorite recipe from: _____

Ingredients: _____

_____

_____

_____

_____

_____

Method: _____

_____

_____

_____

_____

_____

_____

_____

_____

_____

_____

Favorite recipe: _____

Favorite recipe from: _____

Ingredients: _____

_____

_____

_____

_____

_____

_____

Method: _____

_____

_____

_____

_____

_____

_____

_____

_____

_____

Favorite recipe: _____

Favorite recipe from: _____

Ingredients: _____

_____

_____

_____

_____

_____

Method: _____

_____

_____

_____

_____

_____

_____

_____

_____

_____

_____

Favorite recipe: _____

Favorite recipe from: _____

Ingredients: _____

_____

_____

_____

_____

_____

Method: _____

_____

_____

_____

_____

_____

_____

_____

_____

_____

My Favorite Recipes

Favorite recipe: _____

Favorite recipe from: _____

Ingredients: _____

_____

_____

_____

_____

_____

Method: _____

_____

_____

_____

_____

_____

_____

_____

_____

_____

_____

My Favorite Cookie Exchange

Date: _____

Occasion: _____

_____

Guests: _____

_____

_____

_____

_____

Recipes: _____

_____

_____

_____

_____

_____

_____

_____

_____

_____

Date: _____

Occasion: _____

_____

Guests: _____

_____

_____

_____

_____

Recipes: _____

_____

_____

_____

_____

_____

_____

_____

_____

_____

_____

_____

My Favorite Take-Along Treats

Date: _____

Occasion: _____

_____

Guests: _____

_____

_____

_____

Menu: _____

_____

_____

_____

_____

_____

_____

_____

_____

_____

Date: _____

Occasion: _____

_____

Guests: _____

_____

_____

_____

_____

Menu: _____

_____

_____

_____

_____

_____

_____

_____

_____

_____

Date: _____

Occasion: _____
_____

Guests: _____
_____
_____
_____
_____

Menu: _____
_____
_____
_____
_____
_____
_____
_____
_____
_____
_____

Date: _____

Occasion: _____
_____

Guests: _____
_____
_____
_____

Menu: _____
_____
_____
_____
_____
_____
_____
_____
_____
_____
_____
_____

Friend: _____

Date: _____

Cookie gift: _____

_____

_____

_____

_____

_____

_____

_____

_____

_____

_____

_____

_____

_____

_____

_____

My Favorite Cookie Gifts

Friend: _____

Date: _____

Cookie gift: _____

_____

_____

_____

_____

_____

_____

_____

_____

_____

_____

_____

_____

_____

_____

_____

_____

_____

_____

_____

Friend: _____

Date: _____

Cookie gift: _____

_____

_____

_____

_____

_____

_____

_____

_____

_____

_____

_____

_____

_____

_____

_____

_____

_____

_____

Friend: _____

Date: _____

Cookie gift: _____

_____

_____

_____

_____

_____

_____

_____

_____

_____

_____

_____

_____

_____

_____

_____

_____

_____

Friend: _____

Favorite foods: _____

_____

_____

_____

_____

_____

Don't serve: _____

_____

_____

_____

_____

_____

_____

_____

_____

_____

_____

_____

Friend: _____

Favorite foods: _____

_____

_____

_____

_____

_____

Don't serve: _____

_____

_____

_____

_____

_____

_____

_____

_____

_____

_____

_____

TYPES OF COOKIES

Drop Cookies: Drop cookies are as quick and easy as their name suggests—simply mix the batter as directed and drop it by the spoonful onto a baking sheet. Use one spoon to scoop the batter and another to push it off, spacing the cookies about 2 inches apart. Try to make them all about the same size and shape for more even baking.

Bar Cookies: These cookies are a snap to make. Bar cookies only require preparing the batter and spreading it in the pan. For best results, be sure to use the pan size called for in the recipe, otherwise the texture will be affected. Grease the pan only if the recipe directs—some cookies don't need it. Once they have cooled, bar cookies can be cut into squares, rectangles, diamonds and triangles.

Refrigerator Cookies: Refrigerator cookie dough is shaped into a log and chilled until firm before slicing and baking. After shaping the dough, wrap the log securely in waxed paper or plastic wrap, then refrigerate. When firm, slice the dough using a sharp knife and a gentle sawing motion, rotating the log occasionally to keep one side from flattening.

Shaped Cookies: This cookie dough is easily formed into balls, logs or crescents with your hands. The cookies can then be decorated before baking. Simply roll in sugar, top with candies or jam, or flatten with a cookie stamp or fork.

Rolled Cookies: This dough must be chilled and then rolled out on a lightly floured surface. Use any kind of cookie cutter to cut out fun shapes. For best results, dip the edge of the cookie cutter in flour and press down firmly to cut out the dough.

• Read the entire recipe before you begin to be sure you have all the necessary ingredients and utensils.

• Remove butter, margarine and cream cheese from the refrigerator to soften, if necessary.

• Adjust oven racks and preheat the oven. Check oven temperature with an oven thermometer to make sure the temperature is accurate.

• Toast and chop nuts, and melt butter and chocolate before preparing batter or dough.

• Always use the pan size suggested in the recipe. Prepare pans as directed.

• Choose cookie sheets that fit in your oven with at least 1 inch on all sides between the edge of the sheet and the oven wall.

• Grease cookie sheets only when the recipe recommends it; otherwise, the cookies may spread too much.

• Measure the ingredients accurately and assemble them in the order they are listed in the recipe.

• When baking more than one sheet of cookies at a time, it's best to rotate them for even baking. Halfway through the baking time, rotate the cookie sheets from front to back, as well as from the top rack to the bottom rack.

• Always check for doneness at the minimum baking time given in the recipe.

General Substitutions

If you don't have:	Use:
1 teaspoon baking powder	½ teaspoon baking soda plus ¼ teaspoon cream of tartar
½ cup firmly packed brown sugar	½ cup sugar mixed with 2 tablespoons molasses
1 cup buttermilk	1 tablespoon lemon juice or vinegar plus milk to equal 1 cup (stir; let stand 5 minutes)
1 ounce (1 square) unsweetened baking chocolate	3 tablespoons unsweetened cocoa plus 1 tablespoon shortening
3 ounces (3 squares) semisweet baking chocolate	3 ounces (½ cup) semisweet chocolate morsels
1 whole egg	2 egg yolks plus 1 teaspoon cold water
1 cup cake flour	1 cup minus 2 tablespoons all-purpose flour
1 cup honey	1¼ cups granulated sugar plus ¼ cup water

Common Weights and Measures

½ tablespoon = 1½ teaspoons

1 tablespoon = 3 teaspoons

¼ cup = 4 tablespoons

⅓ cup = 5 tablespoons plus 1 teaspoon

½ cup = 8 tablespoons

½ pint = 1 cup or 8 fluid ounces

1 pint = 2 cups or 16 fluid ounces

1 quart = 4 cups or 2 pints or 32 fluid ounces

1 gallon = 16 cups or 4 quarts

1 pound = 16 ounces

Great-looking cookies go a long way toward making an ordinary day extra-special. Try any of the following ideas to jazz up your cookies, bars and brownies.

Chocolate Drizzle

Melted chocolate or white chocolate provides a pretty finishing touch to many baked goods. Simply drizzle melted chocolate with a spoon or fork over baked goods. The contrast of a white chocolate drizzle on a dark chocolate cookie is sure to draw attention.

Powdered Sugar Glaze

Plain cookies get a boost of sweetness with a powdered sugar glaze. Use the glaze white, or tint it with food coloring to fit the occasion. Simply combine 1 cup sifted powdered sugar and 5 teaspoons milk in a small bowl. Add ½ teaspoon vanilla extract or other flavoring, if desired. Stir until smooth and tint with food coloring, if desired. If the glaze is too thin, add additional powdered sugar; if it is too thick, add additional milk, ½ teaspoon at a time.

Toasted Nuts

A sprinkle of chopped nuts is a great topping for frosted treats. To toast, spread nuts in a thin layer on an ungreased cookie sheet. Bake in a preheated 325°F oven 8 to 10 minutes or until golden, stirring occasionally to promote even browning and prevent burning. Toasted nuts will darken and become crisper as they cool. Always allow nuts to cool before using.

Toasted Coconut

Coconut sprinkled on frosted brownies or cookies adds a distinctive appearance and flavor. To toast coconut, spread a thin layer of flaked coconut on a cookie sheet. Bake in a preheated 325°F oven 7 to 10 minutes. Shake the pan or stir the coconut occasionally during baking to promote even browning and prevent burning.

Tinted Coconut

Tinted coconut is a festive decoration for bar cookies. To tint coconut, dilute a few drops of liquid food coloring with ½ teaspoon milk or water in a small bowl. Add 1 to 1⅓ cups flaked coconut, and toss with a fork until it is evenly tinted.

There are several methods for melting chocolate. They all begin with utensils that are completely dry. Moisture, whether from utensils or an accidental drop of water, causes chocolate to "seize," which means it becomes stiff and grainy. If this happens, try adding ½ teaspoon of shortening (not butter or margarine, which contain water) for each ounce of chocolate, and stir until smooth. Also avoid high heat because chocolate scorches easily and once scorched cannot be used. Follow one of these three methods for successful melting.

Double Boiler
This is the safest method because it prevents scorching. Place the chocolate in the top of a double boiler or in a heatproof bowl over hot, not boiling, water; stir until smooth. (Make sure that the water remains just below a simmer and is 1 inch below the bottom of the top pan.) Be careful that no steam or water gets into the chocolate.

Direct Heat
Place the chocolate in a heavy saucepan and melt over very low heat, stirring constantly. Remove the chocolate from the heat as soon as it is melted. Be sure to watch the chocolate carefully because it scorches easily when using this method.

Microwave Oven
Place 4 to 6 unwrapped 1-ounce squares of chocolate or 1 cup of chocolate chips in a small microwavable bowl. Microwave at HIGH 1 to 1½ minutes, stirring after 1 minute. Be sure to stir microwaved chocolate since it may retain its original shape even when melted. It will taste burnt if microwaved after it has melted. Chocolate can also be melted in a small, heavy, resealable plastic food storage bag, turning the bag over after microwaving 1 minute. When the chocolate is melted, knead the bag until the chocolate is smooth. Cut off a tiny corner of the bag and gently squeeze the bag to drizzle the chocolate.

Once you've baked those delicious cookies, you'll want to keep them tasting like they're right out of the oven. To do that, remember the following tips.

• Store soft and crisp cookies separately at room temperature to prevent changes in texture and flavor.

• Keep soft cookies in airtight containers. If they begin to dry out, add a piece of apple or bread to the container to help them retain moisture.

• Store crisp cookies in containers with loose-fitting lids to prevent moisture build-up. If they become soggy, heat undecorated cookies in a preheated 300°F oven for 3 to 5 minutes to restore crispness.

• Store cookies with sticky glazes, fragile decorations and icings in single layers between sheets of waxed paper.

• Bar cookies and brownies may be stored in their own baking pan, covered with aluminum foil or plastic wrap when cool.

• As a rule, crisp cookies freeze better than soft, moist cookies. Rich, buttery bar cookies and brownies are an exception to this rule, since they freeze extremely well.

• Freeze baked cookies in airtight containers or freezer bags for up to six months.

• Thaw cookies and brownies unwrapped at room temperature.

• Meringue-based cookies do not freeze well, and chocolate-dipped cookies will discolor if frozen.

When you can't be with the ones you love, bake them some cookies! And keep the following tips in mind when shipping those special treats.

• Prepare soft, moist cookies that can handle jostling rather than fragile, brittle cookies that might crumble.

• Brownies and bar cookies are generally sturdy but it is best not to ship any with moist fillings and frostings, since they become sticky at room temperature. For the same reason, shipping anything with chocolate during the summer, or to warm climates, is also risky.

• Wrap each type of cookie separately to retain flavors and textures. Cookies can also be wrapped back-to-back in pairs with either plastic wrap or foil.

• Bar cookies should be packed in layers the size of the container, or they can be sent in a covered foil pan as long as the pan is well-cushioned inside the shipping box.

• Place wrapped cookies as tightly as possible in snug rows inside a sturdy shipping box or container.

• Fill the bottom of the shipping container with an even layer of packing material. Do not use popped popcorn or puffed cereal, as it may attract insects. Place crumpled waxed paper, newspaper or paper toweling in between layers of wrapped cookies. Fill any crevices with packing material, and add a final layer at the top of the box.

• Ship the container to arrive as soon as possible.

Metric Conversion Chart

VOLUME MEASUREMENTS (dry)

1/8 teaspoon = 0.5 mL
1/4 teaspoon = 1 mL
1/2 teaspoon = 2 mL
3/4 teaspoon = 4 mL
1 teaspoon = 5 mL
1 tablespoon = 15 mL
2 tablespoons = 30 mL
1/4 cup = 60 mL
1/3 cup = 75 mL
1/2 cup = 125 mL
2/3 cup = 150 mL
3/4 cup = 175 mL
1 cup = 250 mL
2 cups = 1 pint = 500 mL
3 cups = 750 mL
4 cups = 1 quart = 1 L

VOLUME MEASUREMENTS (fluid)

1 fluid ounce (2 tablespoons) = 30 mL
4 fluid ounces (1/2 cup) = 125 mL
8 fluid ounces (1 cup) = 250 mL
12 fluid ounces (1 1/2 cups) = 375 mL
16 fluid ounces (2 cups) = 500 mL

WEIGHTS (mass)

1/2 ounce = 15 g
1 ounce = 30 g
3 ounces = 90 g
4 ounces = 120 g
8 ounces = 225 g
10 ounces = 285 g
12 ounces = 360 g
16 ounces = 1 pound = 450 g

DIMENSIONS

1/16 inch = 2 mm
1/8 inch = 3 mm
1/4 inch = 6 mm
1/2 inch = 1.5 cm
3/4 inch = 2 cm
1 inch = 2.5 cm

OVEN TEMPERATURES

250°F = 120°C
275°F = 140°C
300°F = 150°C
325°F = 160°C
350°F = 180°C
375°F = 190°C
400°F = 200°C
425°F = 220°C
450°F = 230°C

BAKING PAN SIZES

Utensil	Size in Inches/Quarts	Metric Volume	Size in Centimeters
Baking or Cake Pan (square or rectangular)	8×8×2	2 L	20×20×5
	9×9×2	2.5 L	23×23×5
	12×8×2	3 L	30×20×5
	13×9×2	3.5 L	33×23×5
Loaf Pan	8×4×3	1.5 L	20×10×7
	9×5×3	2 L	23×13×7
Round Layer Cake Pan	8×1½	1.2 L	20×4
	9×1½	1.5 L	23×4
Pie Plate	8×1¼	750 mL	20×3
	9×1¼	1 L	23×3
Baking Dish or Casserole	1 quart	1 L	—
	1½ quart	1.5 L	—
	2 quart	2 L	—

Acknowledgments

The publisher would like to thank the companies and organizations listed below for the use of their recipes and photographs in this publication.

Blue Diamond Growers®

ConAgra Grocery Products Company

DAVIS® Baking Powder

Dole Food Company, Inc.

Duncan Hines® and Moist Deluxe®
are registered trademarks of Aurora Foods Inc.

Eagle® Brand

Egg Beaters®

Fleischmann's® Original Spread

Hershey Foods Corporation

HONEY MAID® Honey Grahams

Kahlúa® Liqueur

Kellogg Company

Kraft Foods Holdings

©Mars, Inc. 2001

OREO® Chocolate Sandwich Cookies

PLANTERS® Nuts

The Procter & Gamble Company

The Quaker® Oatmeal Kitchens

The J.M. Smucker Company

Sunkist Growers

Wisconsin Milk Marketing Board

Index